Report Writing for Social Workers

Report Writing for Social Workers

JANE WATT

Series editors: Steve Keen and Keith Brown

Los Angeles | London | New Delhi
Singapore | Washington DC

www.learningmatters.co.uk

Los Angeles | London | New Delhi
Singapore | Washington DC

www.learningmatters.co.uk

Learning Matters
An imprint of SAGE Publications Ltd
1 Oliver's Yard
55 City Road
London EC1Y 1SP

SAGE Publications Inc.
2455 Teller Road
Thousand Oaks, California 91320

SAGE Publications India Pvt Ltd
B 1/I 1 Mohan Cooperative Industrial Area
Mathura Road
New Delhi 110 044

SAGE Publications Asia-Pacific Pte Ltd
3 Church Street
#10-04 Samsung Hub
Singapore 049483

Editor: Luke Block
Production controller: Chris Marke
Project management: Swales and Willis Ltd,
Exeter, Devon
Marketing manager: Tamara Navaratnam
Cover design: Wendy Scott
Typeset by: Swales & Willis Ltd, Exeter, Devon
Printed by: MPG Books Group, Bodmin, Cornwall

Library of Congress Control Number:
2012950813

British Library Cataloguing in Publication Data

A catalogue record for this book is available from
the British Library

ISBN 978 1 44625 710 4
ISBN 978 0 85725 983 7 (pbk)

Dedication

With my heartfelt gratitude and love to Amy and Marley; this book would not have been completed without their strong encouragement and support during a difficult time in all our lives.

Contents

Preface to the Post-Qualifying Social Work Practice Guide Series

All texts in the Post-Qualifying Social Work Practice Guide series have been written by people with a passion for excellence in social work practice. They are primarily written to help social work practitioners in their day to day roles, but they will also be useful for any social worker undertaking more formal professional development.

The books in this series will also be of value to social work students as they are written to inform, inspire and develop social work practice.

We trust you find this text of real value to your practice as a social worker and that this, in turn, has a real impact on those we serve.

Steve Keen and Keith Brown
Bournemouth University

Chapter 1
Introduction

CHAPTER OBJECTIVES

In this chapter, we'll look at:

- how the book is arranged;

- the features and methods which are common to every chapter, and are intended to encourage and facilitate positive development;

- the intentions behind this book and how it will benefit social work staff;

- why reports are regarded as so challenging;

- the positive aspects of report preparation.

This initial chapter is intended to 'set the scene' for the book, showing how it might work for you at different times in your social work career. You will be encouraged to think about how prepared *you* are for this particular type of work, and what you might take from this book to increase your knowledge, experience and confidence.

About this book

Who is this book for?

This book is intended for anyone in social work who has to produce written reports. While it may be of most use to those who have quite recently qualified and who are faced with having to write a report with little or no previous experience of the process, I hope that it'll also be helpful to:

- students who are able to become involved in report preparation in practice learning situations;

- unqualified workers who may have to contribute to reports prepared and presented by qualified colleagues;

- experienced report writers looking for new/different approaches – we are all responsible for our own ongoing learning and development, and for refreshing our existing skills whenever possible;

- any formal or informal training and support groups in the workplace, such as newly qualified groups or report 'gate-keeping' panels;

- those responsible for writing reports on other staff members, such as students, trainees and supervisees;

- anyone who has got stuck on a particular report – writers' block doesn't only affect creative fiction authors!

Book layout

The book is arranged in nine chapters of around 4500 words each and an Afterword. Each chapter will open with an outline of what will be addressed and go on to offer information arranged in short clearly headed sections, of a length to encourage progressive learning and also to consult as and when required.

Each chapter also has a number of practical features, which include the following:

Case Studies: These are examples which illustrate an aspect of a subject under consideration. They are situations I've been involved with or heard about, in both my working and personal life. I hope the case studies will give a sense of everything being 'grist to the mill' and show that the knowledge and experience we draw upon in our social work aren't necessarily just related to our work involvement.

Activities: These are intended as ideas for personal reflection or as discussion starters. Given the pressures of social work, it might be unrealistic to think that a worker who has a report to prepare will have time during that preparation to undertake these Activities. However they may provide a quick extra perspective on a current issue, and can form a base to work from when extending skills and knowledge.

Report Examples: These are sentences or paragraphs taken from social work reports to demonstrate a point or to highlight a dilemma in report writing in social work contexts.

Comments: These sections will offer a bit more detail and discussion of the Report Examples, Case Studies and Activities, and will give you scope to reflect on what you have been asked to do, or to think about.

Practitioner Comments: I have incorporated the written thoughts of a current social work practitioner, Anna Woodruff, which offer the perspective of someone involved in report writing on a day-to-day basis. Practitioner Comments vary from brief comments on points raised by the text to a few paragraphs on a particular aspect.

ANNA'S INTRODUCTION TO HERSELF

I am a social worker in an adult care team/community team. As of last year we became part of a new health and social care social enterprise. I work mainly with older adults, although we are seeing an increase in referrals for younger disabled people and those with complex challenging needs and behaviour. I have been qualified for six years and have just completed my PQ in specialist social work with adults

When I was asked to provide some practitioner reflections for this book, one of my first emotions was shock as it dawned on me that I had not given the subject of report writing a

---

> *great deal of 'reflection' in my social work training or career. Which is ironic, as report writing and paperwork takes up approximately 60–70 per cent of my social work time. When I first started my job, I tried to use some of the skills I had drawn on to write essays, and I remember reading the reports of other team members. That's basically how I learnt to write our reports, which consist mainly of Community Care Assessments, Personal Budget Support Plans and funding applications. Apart from one day's very good legal training, peer support and good management (all, or some of which, people may not always get), there seems to be a lack of focus on this issue in the academic world and in practice in general. That is why I feel the nature and content of this book is really relevant to anyone in practice and why the title of this book challenged me before I even opened the first page.*

Self-Care Tips: Throughout the text I will offer some simple suggestions about looking after yourself while organising and carrying out your work. These will often just be reminders of simple practices which, I hope, you will probably already be following.

These practical features are intended to extend your reflection and learning in a way that is positively beneficial to your practice and role confidence. They can be used as much or as little as is useful (or as you have time for) at present. So do skip them if necessary, but consider returning to them later.

Chapter Review: This will be a brief summary of the work of the chapter and how it will lead into the following one. This section will also list some of the main social work skills referred to in that chapter. This is intended to demonstrate that you already possess the necessary basic skills; naming them will help you acknowledge them and will encourage you to practise and develop them consciously.

Further Reading: Each chapter will end with suggestions and possibilities for extending some of these elements:

- your experience and understanding of life situations;
- your exploration of the practical skills referred to;
- your knowledge of the social work theories and methods that you use in your practice.

This may be in the form of:

- books;
- articles;
- websites;
- people/roles you could seek out as potential sources of information and development.

There is also a Bibliography, listing books which have influenced my writing, even if they are not explicitly referred to in the text.

Book terminology

It took some time to decide upon some of the terms that I've chosen to use. I'll not go into all those debates now, but I would say that regular reconsideration of old issues does ensure reflection upon some vital subjects and the philosophies behind our profession. An example is the question of how to refer to the people with whom you're working:

- In the particular issue of report preparation for a court, there may be differing views about who is the 'client'.

- The term 'service user' might be imagined to imply that a person has chosen to use my agency to write a report about them, which might be far from the truth.

I have chosen to use the term 'client', but Anna has used the term 'service user' in her practitioner comment sections.

Why write this book?

I believe that, as social workers become more conscious of their skills, experience and knowledge, they become more able to demonstrate and develop these. These skills include the vital ones of writing and presenting reports.

My interest in writing this particular book started a long time ago. Over a number of years I was involved in examining samples of Post Qualifying Social Work Portfolios. I became concerned that, all too often, social workers' 'reports' explaining their involvement, assessments and considerations in mental health cases barely reached – or even failed to reach – the required standards.

I found it especially worrying that, from case records and documents, it was clear that most social work was at least satisfactory and often excellent. Some clearly skilled workers were failing to acknowledge their considerable social work competency or to draw out the principles and theories behind their own functioning.

I will encourage you to acknowledge, use and extend your skills to the full, and to do this in a conscious way so that you can explicitly refer to them in reports. I embrace

> the idea that critical thinking can be developed and embedded within existing practice abilities in order for a practitioner to deal confidently with an uncertain and ever-changing world.

> (Rutter and Brown, 2012, pxv)

My approach in writing this book

I adopt a *coaching approach* to staff development. For me, this means helping people to bring out the best of themselves in their work, and to extend their practice through reflection on their own and others' learning and experiences. I believe that we all have a lot to offer one another, even if initially we don't always realise this. Coaching is also about working alongside someone, offering support, and identifying sources of active encouragement, help and further learning potential. It encourages confidence in the acceptance of your skills.

This coaching approach entails my using a style of writing as if I were talking to you, the reader, in a workshop or in a consultancy session on report preparation. Of course, because I'm writing rather than actually speaking to you, it will be edited carefully so that, although I'll use a less formal style than you might be used to in a more 'academic' book, it will hopefully read much more fluently than if I were actually speaking to you! And because I'm writing rather than speaking, we can't have a dialogue about our ideas.

I'd like the book to be used *interactively.* A book might appear to be a very one-sided tool, but I'd encourage you to 'Communicate; collaborate; cooperate and share' (taken from a dictionary of synonyms) the ideas and exercises described here. You could (and, I hope, will) use some of the contents to initiate and inform discussions with a colleague or with a group, such as a group for newly qualified social workers (NQSWs).

Many of the activities and points raised are open to differing responses; there are rarely any completely right or wrong answers in social work, but through intelligent and open discussion, creative and practical ways forward can usually be found.

My writing style will also demonstrate that your words will be more effective if they reflect your audience's needs and your relationship with them. So this book's style wouldn't be the style to use in writing a report. For instance the use of contractions (e.g. 'don't' for 'do not'; 'I'd' for 'I would'; etc.) are inappropriate in a social work report – as are 'e.g.' and 'etc.'!

This will be a *practice-based book* about using and developing already acquired skills to create good reports. A positive approach will demonstrate that reports need not be a frightening prospect, but rather the situation to practise and display the results of the writer's skills. I'll encourage frequent reflection to recognise known skills, to develop confidence and to grow in the professional role.

Many books on social work practice concern the translation of theory into that practice. You'll already have worked on theories and methods to a greater or lesser extent before having to prepare a report. I hope that your interest will be re-aroused and prompt you to revisit theories and methods studied in training courses, using texts you amassed during those courses and current websites, without having to spend additional time or money on acquiring books. This revisiting is an integral part of the reflection that I'd encourage as often as possible.

Apart from encouraging development of social work skills, I will offer practical tips intended to free you from some everyday concerns (such as security of papers and information) so that you can concentrate on the challenging task of report writing.

The book has been written carefully with the new Professional Capabilities Framework for Social Workers in England in mind, and will help you to develop the appropriate standards at the right level.

Chapters

I'll start with some background to report preparation in social work, and a consideration of some fundamental wider issues – ethics, power, social aspects, political aspects, and so on (Chapter 2). Then a stage-by-stage practical approach will be followed through, emphasising the skills to be depended upon at each step, against a background of these fundamental considerations. So, Chapter 3 will be on Getting Started, Chapter 4 on Planning and Timetabling,

Chapter 5 on Interviews, Chapter 6 on Writing, Chapter 7 on Proofreading and Checking, Chapter 8 on Presentation and Chapter 9 will sum up and suggest further ways forward. A short Afterword will sum up my hopes for the book and suggest a couple of simple ideas to inform future practice and development.

What is a report?

The meaning of the word *report* can vary depending upon context.

The Shorter Oxford English Dictionary (1973, p1799) suggests:

> *an account brought by one person to another, especially of some matter specially investigated.*

and

> *a formal statement of the results of an investigation, or of any matter on which definite information is required, made by some person or body instructed or required to do so.*

My computer's 'built-in' dictionary offers these short definitions:

1. account of something

2. news item

3. document giving information

4. unconfirmed account

5. periodic statement of company's finances

6. same as report card

While the *Encarta Dictionary* (2009) from the USA suggests:

> *a document that gives information about an investigation or a piece of research, often put together by a group of people working together.*

Interestingly, few definitions specify that a report must be written – this is given as a likely option. However, in social work and in this book, we use the word to refer only to a written document.

It's in this essential that the social worker may become a little wary; moving from speech into writing changes the status of the information or opinion given.

Who writes reports?

Producing reports can be a major part of the day-to-day work of a great many professions; for instance, surveyors write reports for potential house purchasers; an insurance assessor may write a report on damage in an office following flooding; and teachers may write school reports for students and their parents/guardians.

Do you think there are considerations which you have to keep in mind when tackling a social work report which you think might not apply to other professions?

Comment

The following comments from The Guardian's *Joe Public blog may help your reflection upon this:*

> *What was highlighted by the death of Baby Peter was the considerable competence required of social workers. It showed how amid family chaos and deceit social workers have to seek out and make sense of often conflicting and incomplete information and then make major life determining decisions.*
>
> *Social workers need highly tuned investigative and critical appraisal skills which demand intelligence and imagination. They also need to be in work settings which encourage reflection and review, and with supervisors who are both supportive and challenging. They need time and space, too often lacking in the hurly-burly of busy teams and unstable organisations.*

(Jones, 2009)

Standards of literacy in social work

It's hardly surprising that some student social workers have difficulty with their academic assignments and, once they're qualified, it's difficult to ask for (and to find) help with the actual *writing* part of their job.

Employers are concerned that workers have social work skills (interviewing, analysing situations, and so on), but have less often looked at the ability to write clearly and correctly when demonstrating those skills. It has been taken for granted that, if you've passed a course, you must be able to write well. Most social workers have good verbal skills; they are used to organising information and finding an understandable way of expressing it orally to a wide variety of people. They will usually have the skills to prepare well for interviews and any literacy difficulties may not be apparent.

This area of concern is now being tackled, both in pre-course testing and in standards required for registration. A *Community Care* article, 'Improving Social Workers' Literacy', states:

> *Literacy problems among students have been highlighted in high-profile reviews, including the Social Work Task Force report in December 2009, which noted 'acute concern that a minority of those accepted onto courses have poor skills in literacy or have difficulty in analysing and conceptualising'. 'It is a long-standing issue' confirms Jonathan Parker, Professor of Social Work at Bournemouth University.*
>
> *Bournemouth now expects prospective students to do written and verbal tests, as well as a presentation, to assess their all-round literacy.*

(Gillen, 2011)

Written communication is also listed in the *Standards of Proficiency for Social Workers in England*, which describes:

> what a social worker must know, understand and be able to do when they start practising for the first time.

The following two points are included under Standard 8, headed 'Be able to communicate effectively':

> 8.8 be able to communicate in English to the standard equivalent to level 7 of the International English Language Testing System, with no element below 6.51.

> 8.11 be able to prepare and present formal reports in line with applicable protocols and guidelines.

(Health and Care Professions Council, 2012)

The first of these (8.8) shows that some concerns have arisen due to the increased number of social workers from other countries whose command of English has not been subject to a formal, standardised test. The second (8.11) is intended to ensure that all reports are fit for their intended purpose.

While these changes will hopefully improve standards of writing in social work in the future, they may not help those who currently experience difficulties.

Report preparation is a challenging arena

> There has been a long-term appetite in the media to portray social workers in ways that are negative and undermining.

(Laming, 2009)

It's easy to do a Google search and find many critical statements about social workers' work in reports from the press, politicians and the public. However, it's much harder to 'Google' for praise! Praise seems concentrated upon the work of government-commissioned investigations and reports. The few appreciative comments on social workers I found when doing this exercise were mainly press releases from local authorities praising their particular departments in response to the World Social Work Day held in March each year.

Of course, the many appreciative comments, made in arenas such as care proceedings or Mental Health Tribunals, cannot be reported or recorded. The general public rarely get the chance to understand and appreciate the complex and skilled work of social workers. Professional social work staff are fully aware that they're likely to be 'damned if they do and damned if they don't'.

In a review of a book looking at the power of such publicity (Wendy Fitzgibbon's *Probation and Social Work on Trial*), Guilfoyle talks of a 'hyped up media furore' and states that:

> agencies have been at times held hostage to some of the more hostile political reactions that have reshaped and distorted the practice landscape for front line staff.

(Guilfoyle, 2012)

This general misunderstanding of the role and practical functioning of social work can create apprehension in situations where social workers need confidence to concentrate on using their considerable skills, knowledge and experience. The difficulties of being in an apparently unappreciated, or even denigrated, profession can be distracting, to say the least. However, if a social worker has a confident belief in the integrity and efficacy of the profession and is secure in the value of their own training, skills and experience in that profession, they are freed to devote their considerable skills and intelligence to the challenging task.

Report writing can cause stress for social workers for many other reasons. The writer may be extremely experienced, but when you work with people, no two situations are ever the same. Everyone is different; situations may be constantly changing; relationships and temperaments are dynamic. To remain centred in this often turbulent world requires a mature outlook and a range of skills. Fortunately, all the necessary skills should have been worked on during training and your agency will hopefully have an organised approach to consolidation for NQSWs.

Even for the experienced social worker, the allocation of a new report situation can create apprehension, and complacency can lead to mistakes.

Report writing, often for a little known formal arena such as a court, can be feared because it may seem like a personal exposure of background and basic skills. Where opinions are exposed in writing, vulnerability and insecurity in professional identity may arise.

You can do it

The report preparation task can initially seem overwhelming, but you do have most of the necessary skills. Preparing a report is a distillation of these within a set framework. This book will remind you of required skills and help to develop them in context. The Activities are intended to aid this process.

The overall task will be broken down into stages which will be considered in a logical sequence in the following chapters.

I encourage you to remember what you're doing and why. Reflect positively on your life experiences and become conscious of all the skills you possess. Not only do you have skills based upon training, theory and research, but also others you've absorbed by 'osmosis' from experience and education. Examples include concepts learned from other people met on courses, from practice/observation placements, life experiences and also other learning and training which wasn't necessarily aimed at social work.

References to report preparation situations in this book will usually concentrate on court reports because these often cause most anxiety amongst authors, but the same basic organisation and principles will apply to almost any report, even when prepared by a worker from a profession other than social work.

Are you ready?

It's not only social workers who may need help in the area of report writing and presentation. Other professions see the necessity of offering help to their practitioners too. For instance there is:

a two-day training programme for final year paediatric registrars and newly appointed consultant paediatricians which was developed by lawyers and paediatricians, drawing on an established course run by the Royal College of Paediatrics and Child Health and local expertise. The programme was delivered in a court setting and led to improved confidence in specific skills. Suggests the need for further evaluation involving objective assessment of court reports and performance in court, using peer review and supervision.

(Solebo *et al.*, 2010)

In an article entitled 'Wigs off, jeans on at the Judicial College', Joshua Rozenberg (**www.guardian.co.uk**, 8 February 2012) describes watching some 'Judge training':

Actors and lawyers play out the sort of challenges a judge may face in any jurisdiction – anything from an aggressive QC questioning a dyslexic defendant to a claimant who is unwilling to remove her niqab while giving evidence – and the judge receives feedback on how well he or she copes.

It's just as useful for the other judges in the room. In the normal course of their work, they never see how another judge conducts a case.

So, do think about how prepared *you* are for this particular type of work, and what you might do to increase your knowledge, experience and confidence.

Chapter review

I've described how this book is arranged and my approach to it.

We've considered the place of writing in our lives and in society generally. We've examined the power of the written word and how this could be intimidating to any profession.

Naturally most social workers will be wary when starting a new report, but this wariness will only lead to more careful attention to detail and better concentration on the task.

And there are a great many positive aspects to the task; it can be a chance to use, assess and demonstrate the value of skills to a wide audience. For example:

- The social worker's *communication skills and experience* have helped a tongue-tied young woman to express her anxieties and the reasons behind her behaviour in a coherent way to a court. Using *patience and empathy*, they've gained her confidence and helped her expression without putting words into her mouth.

- *Assessment skills* are used throughout the process, considering the effects of the situation, the family, the location, previous social work plans and interventions, of available resources, of risk, and so on.

- *Negotiating skills* may be used to produce or devise formal or informal contracts for work.

- *Persuasive skills* are necessary to offer and gain agreement from most parties for realistic creative ways forward.

- The social worker's *writing skills* will enable all parties to gain a greater understanding of the overall situation and the considered evaluations that have been made. Clear, accurate and comprehensible writing will help to ensure that the legal processes operate openly and fairly.

Each of the above points will involve a large range of more specific social work skills which you may be taking for granted and not fully appreciating. In encouraging you to reflect upon your practice, I'm asking you to become more aware of your increasing skills.

Once you do appreciate your increasing skills, I suggest that you take this opportunity to work on extending them in as many aspects as possible.

In Chapter 2, we'll consider the general background considerations that will inform all stages of our report preparations.

FURTHER READING

Trevithick, P (2012) *Social Work Skills and Knowledge*. Third edition. Maidenhead: Open University Press.

I will be referring to social work skills throughout this book. It's helpful to have a good text available to refresh or extend knowledge of these skills as appropriate to you.

Trevithick's text considers eighty skills against the current social and political background. It offers summaries of social work theories and suggestions for further reading, without losing sight of the human and personal bases of social work. This text provides an excellent starting point for reading further about all areas mentioned in this book.

The Standards of Proficiency (PDF) can be downloaded at:

www.hpc-uk.org/assets/documents/10003B08Standardsofproficiency-SocialworkersinEngland. pdf

Rutter, L and Brown, K (2012) *Critical Thinking and Professional Judgement for Social Work*. Third edition. London: Sage/Learning Matters.

If you haven't had time to consider these philosophical aspects in depth previously, then this book will help you to understand these approaches in a clear, practical way. Chapters 2 and 3 on critical thinking and professional judgement are very helpful in paving the way to 'embedding critical thinking and developing holistic critical approaches'.

Chapter 2
General considerations

CHAPTER OBJECTIVES

In this chapter, we'll look at:

- the general background issue of the fundamental place of written information in our society;
- the setting for social work report preparation, including:
  - the personal context;
  - the social context;
  - the political context;
  - the legal context;
  - respect;
  - power;
  - feelings.

Introduction

An up-to-date background appreciation of the wider social environment and the bigger issues is necessary in order to gain clarity about the practical role and duties of the report writer.

Whether the report that you've just been given is the first on your own, or one of many you have completed, it's always worth setting this piece of work in its own unique context. In today's ever more rapidly changing world, the context of social work may vary from one day to the next. An obvious example would be when a new piece of legislation comes into force.

Report preparation requires social workers to be very clear about their role, and writing a report may be the first occasion on which you have had to step into a formal, official and legal role. The process can be uncomfortable, and may be even more so when it is necessary in a family where a less 'official' relationship has already been established.

While we have all reflected upon these issues many times, in a dynamic profession like social work it is essential to keep them fresh in our minds.

Many issues will be referred to again in the following chapters as they arise in the context of more practical details, but here I will try to remain on the 'global' level.

For the sake of clarity, I'm dividing these global issues into human, political, social and legal aspects; however, they do all run into each other and overlap – there are no neat distinctions in the world of social work!

The power of the written word

Writing has a fundamental position in our culture. Teachers and families judge primary school children by their progress in the 3 Rs. And while it's almost acceptable to find arithmetic a bit hard, it is never all right to be bad at reading and writing. Here's an example of this attitude, in a television review in a small magazine:

> *No-one asks you to read out the menu to them at the beginning of a meal, claiming not to be too good at reading, however you may find a certain haste to pass on the clever adding up and dividing needed to work out your share of the bill when all of the yummies are safely in the tummies.*

(Latest 7, 2012)

We are constantly bombarded with statistics about reading and writing at the expected standard of an 11-year-old – but how many of us know what this really means? The news media are quieter on the subject of children's numeracy; I presume that this is because writing is a vital part of communication. In later life, many adults are said to go to extreme lengths to hide their reading and writing difficulties. So, we are aware of the power of writing from an early age.

This is reinforced by phrases such as:

> *'Can you put that in writing, please?'*

This can imply many things; it may mean that the speaker thinks you're making a useful valid comment, which it will be helpful to have recorded to use elsewhere. It may mean that the speaker thinks you're talking rubbish and if you write down your comments, you will realise or admit this. It can be used to intimidate clients and prevent legitimate complaints. The phrase relies upon the implication that, once words are written down, they become more serious and more factual.

People are therefore more cautious about committing something to paper than they are about saying it. This may be because

- they're unsure of their facts and opinions;
- they're unsure of their writing ability;
- they have a difficulty with grammar and spelling, which they fear demonstrates basic inadequacies;
- they feel they'll be exposing a poor education;
- they feel powerless because their perceived lack of expertise at written expression will invalidate their underlying good ideas (see Case Study 2.1).

CASE STUDY **2.1**

This is a common fear in many different jobs. I talked about this to a really wonderful professional 'handyman'. He is someone I admire for his intelligence and creativity in finding suitable working solutions for nearly every practical problem. I'm envious of his talents and skills.

He says he hates producing estimates for work. He feels that his poor writing skills will make the potential client think he's stupid and unable to do the work. He also believes that this sometimes means he's offered very low pay for jobs. He sees writing estimates as an exposure of his poor schooling and inability to communicate in writing. He feels clients will look down on him because of it and that it's bad for his business.

He believes that the best way to deal with this is by making a good initial personal contact with potential customers. He can often make a verbal quotation and then the written quotation is created by his wife and he continues to avoid writing in his contacts with the clients, but still feels shame.

Comment
Social work staff are no different from anyone else in this respect and many have lurking feelings like these. However, we cannot hide so easily from exposing such weaknesses.

Another common phrase emphasising the power of the written word is:

'I read it in the newspapers so it must be true'.

This may cause laughter at the supposed naivety of the speaker, but how many of us are completely sceptical about items we read? Recently, I have heard this concept applied to items found on the Internet, which seems to have taken on the newspapers' role of information dispenser.

We've already defined our reports as being essentially *written* records and analyses, so, as we go into the writing of them, we should always be aware of the possible change in status of the information, and be even more careful about the accuracy of the expressions we use.

Again the power of writing is acknowledged by people in most areas of work; take, for instance, this leader in the *British Dental Journal* (2002):

The power of the written word is considerable. Even today we often tend to take what we read in newspapers, books and journals as being correct and true. We make the assumption the writer has checked the facts, looked at the situation as a whole, done all the homework and written a fair and balanced report, article or story. We do this despite the fact that at times we read about something we understand well and the article is often incorrect and biased.

(Grace, 2002)

Today, we have access to more written information than ever before via the Internet – not only in articles and respected bodies' websites, but also through blogs and comments by anyone who cares to put themselves out there.

More reasons than ever to be wary!

Working in the human and personal world

It's vital that you have considered your social work role and accepted your professional integration into it before you have to present yourself to the people involved in your report preparation. These people will include not only the subject and their immediate family and contacts, but also other professionals from similar (and possibly from very different) organisations. You may have to deal with stereotypes that the clients may have about social workers, but also with those that, say, a general practitioner or a psychiatrist may hold. They too may well have been exposed to some poor reporting about social workers in the media.

Occasionally there will even be a history of difficulties in the understanding of, and working with, the various professions, which may affect you before you are even aware of their existence.

We should never forget that most of the 'components' of our work are human beings. Everyone can be subject to whims, strong beliefs, interpretations, and so on. Relationships, including those involving professionals, are dynamic, yet still need to provide an agreed set of 'facts' upon which plans can be based. In other situations and professions, there will be technical facts which might be disputed but which are measurable and have to be admitted when evidence is provided.

In social work it is rare that we have such certainty. We sometimes use 'techniques', but technical results don't usually follow. There are many psychological and educational tests available, but their results are normally only useful as supporting evidence towards conclusions that we will draw from many other sources, such as direct observation, discussion with contacts, and so on.

We will go on to look at preparing a practical introduction for the role of report writer in Chapter 4, but behind that prepared introduction must lie the more general consideration of that role in society,

The following Practitioner Comment illustrates the difficulties which may be involved in ascertaining even the most basic facts, and the dilemmas that can surround this.

PRACTITIONER COMMENT

Sometimes when we assess people with health issues such as ME/chronic fatigue or even short term memory loss, it is difficult to construct a report when what they tell us sometimes conflicts with what we (or other professionals) observe. This can impact on their eligibility for services.

For instance, I worked with a service user who said she needed support to manage shopping and cleaning as well as some personal care, so we put in a personal assistant (through a personal budget). However, a few weeks later when I phoned the personal assistant to review, they said that they only did a few small domestic tasks and no personal care. This then affected her personal budget and so we had to reduce the service and I had to write in my report that no personal care was required.

PRACTITIONER COMMENT (*CONT.*)

On very rare occasions, a service user has been seen out when they said they were house-bound. We therefore have to liaise with other professionals, such as health staff, to gather more information for the report, to get a balanced view and evidence.

The reverse is also sometimes true for people who have short term memory loss. Often when we meet them, they say that they can manage everything, but then the family brings up evidence of where they have not been able to. Our dilemma then with report writing is how we record this. I feel that we need to do this sensitively and carefully, so as not to make the situation worse and so that we don't frighten the person. Sometimes it may not even be appropriate for them to read the report. However, this is very unusual and goes against principles of sharing openly with service users.

So then, the reasons why we have used our professional judgement to not send the report should be clearly recorded and documented – and perhaps discussed with a line manager. The contents of the report can also cause problems for the family – i.e. if they are saying one thing and the service user is saying the other. Despite this, it is still important to record a conflict of views. The author of the report also needs to bear in mind that it can be very distressing for the service user to see the truth of the situation in black and white and, again, they may disagree with what has been written. In this instance I try to use speech marks to quote what people have said (if appropriate) and include the views of other professionals. It may also be useful to see the service user at different times of the day and with different family members, or on their own, to gain a better picture for the report/assessment.

Once again, the report does need to give an honest account of the person's situation. I have found that practising how to write certain phrases is helpful, as is asking other colleagues and looking at their reports.

The nearest examples of relating social work practice to scientific, measurable outcomes I can think of is when we use Fair Access to Care Services (FACS) criteria to assess whether someone is eligible for services. This usually provides a black and white measurement, i.e. if someone is at substantial or critical risk to themselves or others then we can look to providing care. Most local authorities only use substantial and critical levels now. There are times, however, when because of our humanity (and people change their minds) some people's needs do not fit neatly into the FACS criteria exactly and we have to use professional discretion and the agreement of our manager to do something slightly different.

Another part of 'science' that we sometimes draw on is in research and development, i.e. statistics show that a man in his 80s who is in poor health, smokes, drinks, and is isolated in the community, may not last too long due to self-neglect. We consciously or subconsciously as workers gather this information and make decisions depending on his level of need and risk.

Working in the social and political world

Perhaps more than any other profession, that of the social worker is seen to embody the morals and standards of a society. Politicians and the general public feel entitled to comment upon social work, and probably the place where they believe that they see how it works is in reports. No, not in your carefully crafted report to an adoption process where you can feel that you've helped several people striving towards a satisfactory family life. Nor in any of the other reports that you and your colleagues have to prepare. It's in those more publicised reports on events that come out of enquiries and are widely discussed by politicians, experts and the general public.

I won't go into details here because you're all probably aware of the 'bad press' frequently published about social workers. The Further Reading section offers a small selection of such 'reports'.

ACTIVITY **2.1**

Give responses to these three questions. It will be helpful to discuss your responses with others and to learn their thoughts on the subject.

- *As a social worker, what do I personally believe I represent to the public?*
- *What is a stereotypical view of a social worker? What do my clients think? Are they representative of the general public?*
- *What do I believe that judges, politicians and other influential people think?*

Comment
You might like to ask for examples from family and friends or contacts in other professions.

You may find that local policy will influence the public's view of social workers. For example, some local authorities have a 'One Stop' reception where a 'triage' will take place and the client will (hopefully) be 'signposted' in the direction of the appropriate service, such as housing.

(I have used inverted commas here to show my slight unease at the introduction of what I consider the use of technical language to explain the traditional processes of a reception area.)

This approach may be intended to lessen the stigmatisation of people needing social services' help. For instance, I heard a harassed-seeming young mother with a crying baby in a pushchair and a whining toddler who had to be pulled along telling a shop assistant that she was in a hurry to get to social services before it shut. When the assistant glanced up, she quickly added, 'Oh, not for me – the children aren't usually hard to manage – it's about getting handrails put in at my grandfather's flat'. It seemed that both parties felt that social services were for 'problem families'.

Working in the legal world

Laws underpin every society; they reflect history, philosophy, sociology, politics and much more.

Law is an intriguing subject because it is so basic to our functioning. If you feel you don't know much about where laws come from and how they may affect every part of our lives, do try to find the time to look at some descriptions and explanations (see some basic sources in this chapter's Further Reading section). You may become so fascinated that you decide to go even further into the origins and philosophies!

Although we may think of the law as being very precise and strictly interpreted, its origins are in social life:

> *The life of the law has not been logic; it has been experience. The law embodies the story of a nation's development . . . it cannot be dealt with as if it contained the axioms and corollaries of a book of mathematics.*

> (Oliver Wendell Holmes (1841–1935), quoted at **http://www.lawobserver.co.uk/index.html**)

This might almost have been written about social work, and it's always interesting to consider the interrelation of the two areas.

Law in our daily lives

Law pervades our culture and lives, but we are not often consciously aware of it.

Generally speaking, there are two main branches of law: criminal law and civil law. Most of us come into contact with the formal civil law at some time or other (think of house sales, consumer disputes and so on) and are sometimes proud of our involvement. Formal involvement with criminal law is different; we're unlikely to boast of being publicly accused of a criminal act.

When you reflect upon what the words *law* and *legal* mean to you, you may be surprised to realise how much the laws of the land affect your daily functioning.

Much of the country's law is implicit in the ways that we live. We usually abide by laws without questioning these rules of society. As you get up in the morning, drive your taxed, insured and roadworthy car to work, drop off your children at school, park and enter your office base, and so on, you rarely consider all the laws with which you're complying.

Our society functions by most of its members obeying most of its laws most of the time, and we don't often think about the law until there is some question of non-compliance – for instance, when you remember that your car's MOT certificate will run out next week or when you consider crossing the newly red traffic light a few metres ahead because the children are going to be late for school. We normally use the word law and its derivatives when there is some kind of infringement or conflict. Initially you might think that preparing a court report will provide your first real involvement with the legal system, but is this completely true?

Feelings

Clients' feelings

The process of having a report prepared on them may arouse uncomfortable feelings of self-doubt even in very competent 'innocent' parties. For instance, in reporting upon prospective adopters, the very process of being 'examined' for role suitability in what is a legal formal procedure can arouse feelings of inadequacy. It's vital for the report writer to consider and to work with these feelings.

Some of you will personally have experienced legal processes which have some similarities to social work report situations. For instance, you may have been involved in the ending of a marriage, in contesting a will or even in a neighbour dispute, where legal processes have been invoked.

While these experiences can usefully inform your report preparation practice by allowing you to empathise with and *to make sense of some reactions in your interviewees*, they may also strongly arouse deep-seated personal sensations in you (see Case Study 2.2).

The following Activity should not be undertaken whilst you are in the throes of preparing a report. Rather it's something to consider when you're working on developing your skills.

ACTIVITY *2.2*

Try to identify a situation in which you've come into some sort of conflict with the law. It's unlikely that you have not experienced some type of legal conflict, however trivial it might appear. If you are really unable to bring anything personal to mind, then think of a situation that has arisen for people about whom you care. In this way, you will be able to share some of the deep feelings that legal conflicts can arouse.

Try to examine the situation using these questions:

* *What action did you take to resolve the situation?*

* *How powerful could you be in the identified situations?*

* *Did you feel like a victim of the law?*

Comment

Once you've identified an incident where you've come into conflict with the law, and considered these questions, please try to get inside the feelings that you had at the time and also those you're left with.

This may well be a painful experience, and it would be helpful to undertake this exercise with the support of a colleague or friend.

You may think that there is nothing to fear from your intervention as a report writer, but feelings and emotions are not necessarily logical.

CASE STUDY *2.2*

An example from my own experience took place in the French equivalent of a small claims court.

Basically, a young Frenchman with his own landscaping company had done some paving work for me. It was extremely badly done, a fact confirmed by his father, another artisan, who came to inspect. However the young man took me to court to pay the final 25 per cent of the bill (I had paid 75 per cent of the sum due) before rectifying the job.

In the court papers he stated that I'd paid nothing and so I thought it would be a straightforward process.

I spent many hours preparing a fully evidenced account of the situation, in good French (checked by professional French friends).

I was used to speaking in a variety of English courts, including Crown Courts with their pomp and costume, but that did not prepare me for this experience. All the lawyers wore gowns and sat in the court to await their turn, chatting to one another. Cases were conducted over their heads and it was difficult to hear what was said. The judge whose bench was above the courtroom also sometimes asked a lawyer to come up to talk quietly with him. From the young man's papers, I realised that he had misinformed his lawyer and it was obvious from his own submission that I had paid according to the terms of the contract. The lawyer admitted this to me afterwards, but didn't say anything to the judge who clearly had not read the submissions.

Without going into more details, I admit to being very shaken by the whole experience; I was left with feelings of injustice, humiliation, anger and powerlessness.

I lost a lot of confidence in myself, in the justice system and had to fight down feelings of prejudice against French administration in general. I felt that the whole process had been a cosy joining of all parties against me. Although this was some years ago, I still feel pangs of anxiety, anger and hurt when I think about it. Certainly I feel that my bad experience with the paver was exacerbated by the legal process.

Comment

I offer the outline of this experience to illustrate how most of us have had a life experience which will enable us to begin to understand the complex emotions which subjects of our reports might experience.

I hope that it will help you to appreciate how contact with a legal process can exacerbate feelings of anger, powerlessness and being a victim, and can sow the seeds of future prejudice.

Acknowledging feelings

A blurring between the professional and the personal is not a fault, but does need to be acknowledged and worked with. It may be particularly important in report work due to the deadlines.

There are two aspects to this:

- Being aware of how you are feeling and why, thus being able to work around these reactions to create a balanced, unbiased report.

- You may need to talk over your own feelings, which have been aroused.

It's important from the aspect of worker self-care that there is space for you to work through any difficult feelings which arise during your professional life. Whilst many social workers successfully do this with someone outside their professional situation, this may create difficulties. For instance, a personal partner might start to resent the amount of time that work related issues take up in the home.

Do you acknowledge strong personal feelings which come up during your work? Do you have supervision (or another outlet) to help you to identify which issues arouse feelings and can help you to work with these?

If you haven't already considered this it may be helpful to establish a 'safe' place to consider feelings before undertaking another report. In a challenging arena like social work, we are all liable to be personally affected at some time by the situations we encounter. It's impossible to anticipate every scenario, but you can put in place methods of helping yourself to deal with whatever does come up.

Power

We have already considered the power of the written word generally in Chapter 1, but in considering our power in writing social work reports, we need to be more specific.

You might find it useful to consider some questions posed by David Howe in *A Brief Introduction to Social Work Theory*:

> *Language is the currency of discourse and so great attention is paid to language and how it is used. How do dominant groups talk about those who are relatively powerless? If we alter our language can we alter the way people perceive and relate to one another? Can the words used change the balance of power in relationships?*

(Howe, 2009, p136)

It's vital to understand that your choice of words may carry far-reaching effects.

You do need to be honest, not only with clients but also with yourself, about your power. It can seem a little frightening and even overwhelming when you consider the influence that you can have.

But it can be a very positive influence and power. You have the power to encourage the best possible outcome for certain people and groups. Your carefully worked out plan for a child's future may be accepted and you will have set them on the road to a satisfactory future.

There are other less direct issues of *power*; you will have influence and power in a variety of areas, particularly those that we've already considered above, such as the political, social, policy and organisational areas. This can be at local or occasionally even national levels.

An example might be that you identify in your report that a certain type of facility would be the ideal placement for the client. Unfortunately this type of facility doesn't exist locally and you cannot obtain funding to send them to a suitable unit in another area. In deciding to identify this facility, its appropriateness for your client and its non-availability, you're making a political comment. You may influence the judge you're presenting to. Even if this can't or doesn't result in a comment in open court, it might later lead to that particular judge commenting in a meeting on a committee or even in a more personal arena.

ACTIVITY **2.3**

In the above situation (or a similar one from your own experience):

- *Would you include this possibility in your report, or omit it on the grounds that such an outcome is not possible and so there is no point in mentioning it?*

- *Would it be appropriate to write, 'It's unfortunate that X Local Authority doesn't currently have the Y facility available'?*

- *Or would it be appropriate to write, 'It's unfortunate that X Local Authority doesn't currently have the Y facility available. In Lady A's report to the Government last July, it was recommended that every local authority should make such facilities available in cases assessed as suitable by social services'?*

Comment

If you should find yourself in a situation where you have a dilemma of this sort, please do discuss it thoroughly with someone from the hierarchy of your agency. There may or may not be policies and guidelines in this area of practice, but you do need to be aware of agency practice. This is one of many reasons why reports should be 'gate-kept'. (See also Chapter 7: Checking and Proofreading.) Management also need to be aware of such situations and might ask that the dilemma be omitted from the report, but agree to raise the issue and work towards a resolution through what is considered to be a more suitable channel. It might only be at this point that you are informed of efforts already underway to provide this resource. You are an employee of the agency and it's your job to provide realistic solutions and ways forward. We encourage clients to live in and make the best of the real world, but we too have to do the same and compromise is essential. This may be especially hard for newly qualified workers who feel themselves full of revolutionary zeal and who may find themselves in conflict with the pragmatism of colleagues whom they see as cynical.

It's important to recognise such dilemmas and to practise their resolution for yourself. This can be a very useful topic to discuss with colleagues or groups.

Of course the arena of service delivery isn't always negative; it can be very positive. Where you identify a provision that would be very useful in the given circumstances, you might influence your agency to make arrangements to 'buy in' from somewhere else, or even provide (or look to alter) existing facilities to deliver what is needed on this occasion. Funding shortages can provide opportunities to adapt existing facilities to meet current changing needs. Creative thinking and planning is necessary in social work, and report preparation might provide you with the sharpened focus to work on a particular identified need.

Respect

I hope that from our reflections in this chapter upon general context that it will be clear that the concept and principle of respect should lie behind social work and report preparation. This will entail respect for the institution for which the report is being prepared; respect for the subject(s) of the report; respect for oneself in the role of social worker and respect for oneself as a feeling human being.

Respect is involved:

- in all our communication with all parties;
- in examining our descriptions of situations for any prejudice and discrimination;
- in writing reports in language in the appropriate register for the place they will be presented, but is also clear and simple enough to be understood by readers with differing educational backgrounds;
- and in a great many other activities.

Whilst not always explicitly referred to in the following chapters, it is the basis from which reports should be prepared.

These aspects of *power* and *respect* are intertwined and must be a constant consideration for social workers. The General Social Care Council (GSCC) publication *Professional Boundaries* carries good clear messages about the importance of the relationships between people in the work context, acknowledging 'the considerable harm that professional boundaries violations can have on service users'. However it goes on to show 'the inadvisability of attempting to address this problem through issuing a list of "dos" and "don'ts" ' (p2).

This publication suggests ways of assessing our own actions or potential actions, by considering the following questions on general professional boundaries:

- *Would you be comfortable discussing all of your actions, and the rationale for those actions, in a supervision session with your manager?*
- *Would you be uncomfortable about a colleague or your manager observing your behaviour?*
- *If challenged, could you give an explanation as to how your actions are grounded in social work values?*
- *Do your actions comply with the relevant policies of your employer?*

(GSCC, 2011)

(Note that the regulation of the social work profession and education has now transferred to the Health and Care Professions Council (HCPC).)

This type of questioning is a valuable one when reflecting upon possible action in social work. Whilst there is always the possibility of equivocation in ourselves, we may be more rigorous when we examine a situation through the imagined eyes of others.

Naturally it is the difficult *grey areas* that can give the most concern. It is probably even more so when it is not even our own dilemmas which are an issue, but the attitudes and behaviour of a colleague (or another professional) which is worrying (see Case Study 2.3).

Whilst we now hear of 'whistleblowing' in many areas of life, this is usually related to exposing organisational irregularities, rather than the failings of a colleague.

A social worker (A) was preparing a report for a local family court. In the course of her enquiries, she had to interview the child-minder of the children concerned. This was a positive and pleasant home visit and A was impressed by the warmth and understanding of the child-minder and the positive contribution that she was making to this situation.

However, having got the 'work' of the interview over, she was chatting with the woman and found that the child-minder's daughter was having a personal relationship with another social worker (B) whom she'd met through his visit to the home on another work matter. This was not relevant to the situation upon which A was reporting, but was knowledge which she could not ignore.

By the time that A had arrived back at the office, she was angry and upset. Angry because she felt her colleague B had involved her in a very difficult situation through his self-indulgence and lack of professionalism. Upset because it was quite possible that, once she'd alerted her management to the situation, the equilibrium of the child-minding situation might be disturbed.

A was fortunate that her good relationship with her supervisor enabled her to make a prompt and clear account of her experience. The supervisor then thanked her for her openness and took on the complete responsibility for dealing with the situation, freeing A to continue working on the report.

Comment
While there was no 'urgent abuse' situation here, immediate reporting of this irregular situation was necessary.

What else?

Local Knowledge: There may be other general considerations which you will have in mind during these pieces of work which are particularly pertinent to your agency, your experience or your geographical area. This is where you need to be aware of all the useful knowledge that you've amassed; this contextual knowledge can be more 'down-to-earth' than that considered earlier. For instance, it may be as simple as your particular knowledge of the estate where the client lives.

Access to 'other' situations: While preparing a report, you may have access to homes which are not usually subject to any kind of scrutiny. Such visits or encounters may involve people other than the direct subjects of your report. This can often be a positive experience, offering a view of stable contented functioning lives, to a social worker who has become used to visiting homes which are inhabited by unhappy people lurching from crisis to crisis or those who have been ground into apathetic misery by poverty and despair.

You might then find yourself particularly shocked by observing signs of some sort of abuse in a family you are only visiting because you are preparing a report on someone who has a connection with them. This will bring with it the question of how to deal with what you suspect. While your report interview is not the place to investigate further, it is, of course, possible that your suspicions will be relevant to the report situation.

In any situation, if you have reason to suspect serious abuse of any sort, it will be essential to discuss this immediately (see Case Study 2.4). For example, if you are due to go straight home after this particular visit, do either call at the office on the way, or if this isn't practical, telephone your supervisor or duty person and have a verbal consultation about your concerns. There should be someone available to deal with such issues; it is likely to be highly inappropriate for you to investigate further.

CASE STUDY 2.4

On a Friday afternoon, a student social worker visited a family, known to his supervisor, in order to prepare a report required for an application for some much needed practical aid. This should have been a relatively straightforward task, but the student was concerned to find a very dirty home, a child in a dirty smelly nappy and a four-year-old crying for food. On questioning, the lone mother (C) was very vague and couldn't help the student with facts he needed for the application. She said there was no electricity and no food in the house, but seemed unconcerned about the situation.

The student returned to the office and immediately sought out his practice supervisor who was packing up for the week. She listened to his concerns, and told him that this was typical of C and that she'd probably visit her mother later to get food. She sometimes appeared apathetic because of medication for depression, but would always rouse herself when things got too much. The student was advised to go home and told to check back on C on Monday when he'd see the practice supervisor was right.

The student initially followed this advice, but continued to feel extremely worried and eventually decided to trust his instinct and risk being considered naive and over-anxious; he telephoned the supervisor of practice teachers. This supervisor heard his description of the situation and then contacted an out-of-hours duty worker. This supervisor later phoned the student back at home to thank him for his insistence on reporting the situation; the children had been taken into temporary care as their mother was still not responding satisfactorily, had made no efforts to obtain food and might be admitted to psychiatric care. The duty worker confirmed that the situation should not have been left until Monday. She was appreciative of his clear description of the various aspects of the situation and his assessment of C's condition.

Chapter review

In this chapter we have looked at the wider picture in order to gain clarity about the practical role and duties of the report writer.

These are implicit in social work generally, and particularly in report preparation. These issues will be referred to again in other chapters, but are introduced here to emphasise their place in the structure of social work.

It's important to be aware of them, but they are the just the backdrop and context to your report preparation. Respect for institutions and people will lie behind the practical issues involved in preparing reports.

Particularly relevant social works skills for this chapter are:

- a basic knowledge of the legal framework of our society;

- an understanding of the place of social work in our society and the ability to work with this;

- an understanding of oneself and one's life experiences, and the ability to remain conscious of these while working effectively with others;

- the ability to reflect usefully;

- openness to development and learning;

- the willingness to seek appropriate help;

- keeping up-to-date with current policy, politics and legal and social issues.

Having considered the 'setting' for social work reports, we will go on to more practical issues in the next chapter, looking at organisation and management of paperwork and records.

FURTHER READING

Wacks, R (2008) *Law: A Very Short Introduction*. Oxford: Oxford University Press.

A succinct and clear introduction to the subject of law in general, including history and projections for the future.

Sixth Form Law offers clear information about all basic aspects of English law.

http://sixthformlaw.info/index.htm

Justice is the official government site about the English justice system. Offers an overview of the system, and provides alerts to current media features.

http://www.justice.gov.uk/

Law Observer provides some useful background history to the law.

http://www.lawobserver.co.uk/legal_system_20.html

General Social Care Council (2011) *Professional Boundaries: Guidance for Social Workers*. London: GSCC.

A useful, easy to read publication based upon two research publications into the area of professional relationships. It makes a good discussion starter and, while it cannot offer strict rules, it does contain useful pointers.

Regarding reporting on social work and showing some aspects of its position in society, the following web addresses offer some insights:

The BBC record on the report into the death of Baby P is clearly set out, giving it an 'official' appearance and refrains from comment:

http://news.bbc.co.uk/2/hi/uk_news/7758897.stm

The following two newspaper items show biased reporting and some comments from the public:

http://www.dailymail.co.uk/news/article-2048328/Social-workers-blamed-Gloria-Dwomoh-force-fed-baby-death.html

http://www.telegraph.co.uk/news/uknews/7318789/Timeline-of-social-services-failures-from-Victoria-Climbie-to-Baby-P.html

This *Community Care* debate shows some social workers' opinions about their profession:

http://www.communitycare.co.uk/carespace/forums/-12440.aspx

Chapter 3
Getting started

CHAPTER OBJECTIVES

In this chapter, we'll look at:

- creating the different deadlines needed, whilst respecting the 'official deadline';
- organising your work into a Report File;
- taking account of security of information;
- identifying and sourcing the necessary practical resources;
- how to develop more focused reading of files.

Introduction

We've already looked at the fact that preparing a report is a focused use of your existing social work skills and a good chance to develop and display them. Even if you still feel a little intimidated by the prospect, remember that any task becomes easier if you break it down into comprehensible parts and plan the achievement of each. Chapter 4 will concentrate on getting started by building the framework and planning the timetable for the work. If you've the luxury of preparation time before being allocated your next report, there are suggestions for action in the Further Reading section at the end of this chapter.

First things

So a report request arrives on your desk (or in your in-tray, your e-mail account or other communications system). You may be expecting it (your supervisor discussed it with you earlier, you asked for it at an allocation meeting, it's required for a current client) . . . or it may be a complete surprise.

Probably the first thing you'll notice is whether you personally know the situation and, if not, whether your agency has been involved at some time or this is a completely new situation. We will go on to reflect on these differences and their effects on the work in the next chapter.

The second thing you may notice is the deadline for the report.

Deadlines

There will usually be a clear official deadline, such as the presentation of the report to a court or a meeting. However, you then have to consider other deadline stages before this. You will normally have to create these yourself, working backwards from that final deadline.

Generally you'll need the following:

- A deadline for completing your enquiries and information gathering. You will then select the required contents and start writing the report.

- A deadline for finishing your draft report. You then need to submit the report to your supervisor, a team leader, your legal advisor, a gate-keeping procedure or a report buddy. Perhaps you'll have benefitted from ongoing help during the preparation or perhaps this will be the first time someone else sees it. Whichever it is, this process is really helpful. Even the most perfect report might contain a sentence that isn't quite clear in meaning to an objective reader.

- A deadline for delivering your final version to the person responsible for producing the beautifully set out paper report which will be presented. It's often helpful to discuss this deadline at an early stage with the service responsible for this task, and to agree a date which will allow you time to check the final version carefully before signing it.

It's worth clarifying these deadlines at the outset, as they will form the framework for planning your work. They may also dictate how much time you have for 'extras', such as visiting a Mental Health Tribunal in advance if you are asked to write your first report for one. In Chapter 4 we will go on to timetable contacts and interviews based around these deadlines.

Organisation

Reports can be very complex pieces of work, requiring various items of research, information gathering, discussion and analysis. You may have a great many different sources of information and ways of contacting them. You may collect snippets of information at any moment, and it can be time consuming if you can't find them exactly when you want them.

For example, you don't want to be searching for Mr Jones's child-minder's phone number when you have five minutes to make an appointment to visit, or for that copy of Mrs Smith's criminal record when she's due to arrive at your office to discuss it.

Although you may already be accustomed to using your agency and your own personally developed organisation systems, these may need some honing to maximise your reporting skills.

The Report File

Preparing a report is a finite piece of work and, as such, deserves its own file. A well-organised file will save you precious time and will give you more confidence in your role as report writer.

However, I emphasise the expression 'well-organised'. A large brown envelope full of bits of paper wouldn't work for me!

Tips for creating your own Report File (to be freely adapted to suit *you*):

- A file needs to be of tough material, as it may take a lot of use and some knocks.

- It needs to have pockets for the unavoidable one or two scraps of notes, or you need to be able to punch holes immediately to keep them in a ring binder.

- Number the pages in pencil, so that they can be changed as you progress.

- It will help to keep **a brief running record of your work**, with questions arising/points to follow up recorded in a different colour. If this is the top sheet of the file every time you open it, you will see at a glance where you're up to.

- Record **everything.** For example, you are writing about a child whose grandfather, whom he rarely sees, phones you every day or so. It's annoying when you feel most of these calls are pointless, but they must be recorded. If nothing else, they do show great anxiety about the situation. You may later need to show the contact you've had (in court or in the section of your report recording the sources of your information). This is done quickly by a brief note in your diary, which can later be transferred to the running record.

   So you may need to write in your report, 'John only sees his grandfather, Mr Samuel Smith, once a fortnight or so, but since my home visit to him on December 1st, Mr Smith has phoned me frequently (13 times in six weeks). Mr Smith shows great concern over what is going to happen in John's future.'

SELF-CARE TIP

Your 'diary' may take a paper or electronic form, but should work for you. Use it as a quick record for events throughout the day. Five minutes 'summing up' at the end of the working day, recording everything in the correct place may encourage a more relaxed evening with space to concentrate upon your personal concerns.

Security of information

Once you have your report file, where do you keep it? Security is always of paramount importance. Your work place will have its own rules and policies on the subject and no doubt these are developing as communication methods change rapidly. Of course, you wouldn't take bulging old paper files to a client's house for a routine home visit, but mightn't you be tempted to take your slim neat report file when working on this task? You cannot keep all the necessary information in your head and it's essential to keep your mind clear for really concentrating on the interview (see Case Study 3.1).

CASE STUDY 3.1

A probation officer (Z) travelled by train to a remand prison to interview two different prisoners for court reports. He'd met neither of them before and needed to exploit every minute of the relatively short time allowed with each person so that he wouldn't need to make a repeat visit. He was allocated one hour in the morning with the first man and one hour in the afternoon with the second man.

On the morning train he read up the file and prepared his interview with the first man. All went according to plan and Z had a successful interview with the first prisoner. He had managed to record all the information he needed from this man for his court report.

At lunchtime he had to leave the prison and went to the nearest pub for a sandwich. He took this opportunity to look over the second man's file and prepare his afternoon interview . . . and two sheets of paper slipped out of the folder onto the floor. When leaving the pub, he was 'saved' by the barmaid clearing his plate, who spotted the papers and ran after him.

At the time, Z just thanked her profusely and ran for the prison, knowing that it would take some time to get through the entry formalities before the interview. It was only later as he was sitting in the return train (after running from the prison to catch it) that he allowed himself to reflect upon what had happened.

Even whilst he was berating himself for his carelessness, he realised that he was writing brief notes summing up his last prison interview. He'd taken down the important factual points and the defendant's responses to his questions, but he needed time immediately afterwards to record his impressions and some descriptions before these faded from his memory.

This encouraged him to reflect upon all the factors which had led to his serious slip-up. There were a great many external pressures on him:

- *remand prisoners were held at some distance from Z's office base;*

- *he had **two** remand prisoners to interview;*

- *the usual report writing deadline was further constrained by the need to find a whole day to make his enquiries;*

- *he was using public transport and the train times were not very convenient for the prison visiting times;*

- *the train station was over half a mile from the prison;*

- *he needed to carry some official papers with him to be verified with the prisoners;*

- *in order to be prepared for his two interviews, he had to work both on the train and somewhere at lunchtime;*

- *there were no venues near the prison where he could both eat and work comfortably.*

He came to the conclusion that the various stresses meant that errors were always possible, and that it was not enough to be aware of these constraints: it was necessary to put in place ways of making the situation as workable as possible.

Z brought his experience to a team meeting, where his frankness allowed colleagues to recount similar situations. This enabled the team to highlight this important issue and so to share ideas to prevent these incidents and to create a more vigilant approach to information safety. They also put a standard 'security' item on team meeting agendas to ensure it was always kept in mind.

ACTIVITY 3.1

Can you identify other external constraints on Z?

Can you suggest guidelines for a team (or individual worker) to enable best or 'good enough' practice in such situations?

Comment

It took the horrible shock of realising that he had left important official papers giving personal details of an individual's circumstances in a very public place for Z fully to take stock of the pressures under which he frequently operated.

Fortunately, he was working in a team where he could reveal the incident and they decided to establish a team protocol for such external visits.

The guidelines might include train timetables, basic maps and/or directions from the station to the institution, good places to eat, workers' experiences of reception procedures, and so on. Accepting that train and visiting times might always make the transfer between station and prison difficult means looking at known possibilities and searching for alternatives. And, of course, **it's essential also to keep in mind the needs of less physically able workers***.*

Whilst I've concentrated upon a prison and a city centre in this exercise, similar factors will naturally apply to a wide variety of other situations, such as a children's residential facility in the countryside, sheltered housing in the middle of a large housing estate in another town, and so on.

SELF-CARE TIP

Save stress and anxiety by preparing adequately for visits outside your usual area. Allowing sufficient time to arrive calmly and coolly will set you up for a good visit.

You might already have a personal (or hopefully team or office) file containing such important pieces of information about places you might have to visit. If such a resource already exists, do take time to keep it up-to-date; if there isn't one, think about instigating a discussion towards the creation of this timesaving and confidence boosting item. As time becomes more and more limited, it becomes even more important to share knowledge.

Keeping information secure

- **Try to ensure interviews take place in the office**, so that you rarely need to take out written 'private' information. Office appointments demonstrate that the interviews designated for report preparation may have a more formal status and purpose than a chat at home. Requiring clients to come out for an appointment allows them to show a commitment to the process. However this won't always be possible as in the case of the probation officer above.

- **Prepare the shortest possible list of facts** you need to verify or issues you need to explore. This could be in the form of brief notes at the top of the first page of the note-book you will probably use to record points from the interview. Never keep personal details (such as names and addresses) on the same sheet as other information (such as court orders or hospital admissions). Addresses can be noted in your diary beside the appointment time.

  So, for instance, if you have to take a school report to a home to discuss it with a parent and child, consider making a photocopy with the child's and the school's names blanked out.

  If you have more than one sheet, number them.

- **How do you carry any papers you really must take out?** A satchel style briefcase is often the best solution. It should have a firmly closing top and several file sized compartments, so you can carry information on several different cases if necessary – it's important not to have to take all your papers out of the briefcase each time. You may have several routine home visits to do on the same trip as your report preparation interview. You don't want Ms Jones's hospital report to be on top of Jimmy Clark's tenancy agreement when you take it out to go through it with him in his home.

  Separate compartments can also be used for personal items, such as sandwiches (if out for the day), money, umbrella and so on, without resorting to a handbag. Handbags can be awkward to use for formal A4 size documents, and it looks unprofessional to have folded case papers amongst your son's invitation to the nursery party and your tennis club application. A single multi-purpose bag is easier to keep track of.

- **On leaving an interview room**, wherever it is, always check for coats, scarves, pens and papers.

- **When you're using public transport** it's much easier to look after a single bag; hold it securely under one arm when in crowded conditions. Don't be tempted to study documents if you can't be sure whether anyone else can see them.

- **When using a car**, make sure you lock items out of sight in the boot and keep the lid or parcel shelf in place in a hatchback. Park your car in a safe visible place whenever possible.

ACTIVITY 3.2

1. *What is your organisation's policy on working from home, and is this followed in practice?*

2. *What would you do if you left a work file in a taxi?*

3. *What do you think should happen to a worker who left a work file in a taxi?*

4. *Imagine you are the client whose file was left in a taxi; what would you feel if you found out?*

Comment

You do need to be clear about the local answer to the first question above. It may take some time for you to get to the bottom of what is acceptable in your particular team and then to proceed by getting any necessary clearance for what you want to do. So, if it's usual practice to take old reports out of the office if they are signed out and in again by a supervisor, then do exactly that.

Questions 2 and 3 in this Activity are intended to encourage discussion about data protection in your daily professional life, and you or your colleagues can probably think of similar 'dilemmas' that have occurred in your office which you may find it more helpful to debate. There are no right or wrong answers, but I hope you can come to some agreement about 'best practice'.

The final question is to encourage appreciation of the position of the subject of a social work report, and as a reminder that respect for that person is reflected in every aspect of the work.

Work space

Ideally, you will have a desk in a quiet space, where you can concentrate on reading and writing in these stages of preparing your report. Is there an interview room, a library corner, a training office, a colleague's office or a conference room (which may have a big table that can be used to sort piles of paper) that can be borrowed or booked? If not, think further afield: working at home, the reading room in a public library or even a quiet corner of a local café might be worth considering, but agency policy and security of information must always be of paramount importance.

If all else fails, get some earplugs and some big 'Do Not Disturb' signs!

Materials

Think about how you're going to work and make sure you know how to get stationery items or get a kit ready in advance. It's useful to have coloured pens, pencils and eraser, Post-it stickers, a hole punch, paperclips. Your kit will reflect your chosen way of working.

I like to use different coloured pens to identify different issues, for example, green for people/organisations to contact; blue for facts (such as dates) to verify; red for important events. Of course, highlighters can do the same job. You might also like a pencil (and rubber!) to make notes to yourself on important items on old records or legal documents or to number pages on these records so that you can refer to relevant pages in your notes (such as change of foster family), and so on.

Going through the paperwork

In an old study of social enquiry reports, Fred Perry found that 'the provision of the most basic material . . . was haphazard and unreliable' (Perry, 1974, quoted in Walker and Beaumont, 1981).

More recently, *The Guardian* reported on the Serious Case Review carried out by Sir Christopher Kelly (Chairman of the National Society for the Prevention of Cruelty to Children) into the case of Ian Huntley and the Soham abductions, commenting that 'The report sets out the chaotic state of North East Lincolnshire social services'. It goes on to blame 'poor decision making, bad communication and substandard practice and procedures' (2004).

These findings seem realistic when you look at some old files and reports. Your first reaction might be dismay at the large folder that drops on your desk! It may be full of old files shedding notes and scraps of paper; up-to-date legal documents; a pro-forma document for such reports. Or, it may contain very little and you will have to make a list of what you require and search out missing items.

Training materials on recording (2003) state:

> In their research on parental perspectives on child protection Cleaver and Freeman reported that it was not uncommon for the spelling of the child's name or dates of birth to be incorrect in reports for child protection conferences or court proceedings. This had the effect of undermining parents' confidence in social services.

Naturally, it would not only be the parents' confidence that would be undermined but also that of judges, legal and other professionals and possibly the general public if participants told others of their experiences.

While such errors might initially seem incredible, if you look at a mess of old papers, you might understand a worker copying the first basic 'facts' they come across, not verifying them with the subject(s), and then the mistakes being perpetuated by the next worker. Always check the most basic facts; don't rely on paperwork. **You do have to go through the paperwork; make sure you don't miss bits.**

> When faced with a large, unfocused record practitioners may respond by going prospecting for information. Prospecting practitioners skim through the file. They cannot say at the beginning of their search exactly what information they are looking for, but recognise it when they find it. The danger in this approach is that important information may be overlooked, either because its significance is not appreciated or because it does not conform to the preconceived view held by the practitioner.

> (Monnickendam *et al.* cited in Walker *et al.*, 2012)

A succession of previous reports may just appear to be copies of the original, but sometimes an extra paragraph might have been slipped in to update it. If you find items which really are copies, then place them in a separate marked folder out of your way.

The initial paper sorting is easier if you can beg, steal or borrow the space to have as many piles as you need. For instance, separate piles of legal papers; of school reports; of residential organisation reports; of old records; of inter-agency case conference reports; of medical records; and so on. I find Post-it stickers useful for labelling piles. If you've found a work space, maybe you can use it for your initial sorting. If not, any big table or a quiet bit of floor will make this process quicker and easier.

Once the initial sorting is complete, you can retire with your different categories of papers to read them intelligently, which, again, is done more efficiently if you have space and quiet.

Hopefully you will have identified your work space for doing this, and will have any materials you need. I prefer to use A4 paper for the task as it's large enough to contain several different lists on one side, can easily be photocopied, and fits in files and envelope folders. But do consider whether a reporter's notebook, flipchart paper, laptop or even a whiteboard or voice recorder would suit you better, if they are available. It's important to find tools which are practical for you personally.

Focused reading of old records and other paper information

- Firstly, check pages are in date order, with the latest on top, and are numbered.

- Note only things that are relevant to your task, which includes understanding the essential background.

- Keep your notes succinct and concise.

- A useful method is to create a series of **lists**, maybe on separate sides of paper, which can be added to as you go through the documents. List titles will depend to some extent upon the purpose of the report, but should generally include:

  - The **heading**, which is the document source, for example, social service records from 2003–2007.

  - **'Facts'**, such as dates of birth, addresses, significant people, agencies involved, etc. 'Facts' should always be verified wherever possible. You might be surprised at just how many discrepancies are discovered, even in dates of birth.

  - A general brief **history of events**; for example, births, hospital admissions, changes of social workers, and so on.

  - Any other items that strike you as **relevant in explaining the current situation.**

  - **Points that you can't make sense of.**

Sometimes ploughing through old records seems a tedious and irrelevant task, but it can be surprisingly useful. If nothing else, it may give a sense of the relationships that have existed between the client and your (and possibly other) agencies in the past, and shed some light on seemingly odd decisions.

Even when you don't have to tackle huge piles of paperwork, and when your report is really just a summing up of your current work, it can still be helpful to mark an objective pause to reassess a situation and to perhaps look at it from other perspectives. This can lead to alteration of plans and working methods.

When you've completed the perusal of the paperwork, you should have compiled some lists, such as:

- facts to be verified;

- individuals to contact;

- organisations to contact;

- situations/history to be checked;

- missing information – what more do I need; where can I get it?

The last is perhaps the hardest as it's always difficult to identify what you don't know. So, do think carefully about anything that puzzles you, strikes you as odd or which you just can't make sense of. Is there any way of shedding some light on whatever it is? Perhaps talking over your concerns with a supervisor or colleague will enable you to clarify the issue.

These lists can go in the Report File, ready to be used to plan your timetable and interviews.

The future

It's clear from the Laming Report (2009) that some very serious failures to protect children might have been avoided by better organisation, recording and information sharing in social services and other involved agencies. Lord Laming recommended that the social services computer recording should develop to include the traditional reflective analysis, risk assessment and skills that are often lacking in current information technology.

So I hope that in the future you will not be battling with mounds of sometimes seemingly irrelevant paper and will be aided by more relevant computer systems.

Chapter review

In this chapter, we've looked at the organisation of practical aspects of report preparation. As it's a time-limited task, it's important to create a framework with staged deadlines to work within. Work will always be easier if you've already planned how to go about it and made sure that you have the appropriate equipment and knowledge.

Security of information is a vital aspect of report preparation, as it is of social work in general. It is important not just from the point of view of your legal obligations, but also the respect that you show towards your clients. Please do consider it even in the most mundane aspects of your tasks.

You can concentrate on the important tasks of information gathering, analysis and planning outcomes if you're confident that you already have the more practical aspects, such as space and materials, sorted out.

Your basic task in going through the documents relating to the case is to reduce them and to make sense of them. Doing this thoroughly will clarify your work in planning for interviews, which we'll be looking at in the next chapter.

This chapter mainly calls on the use of your

- personal and work organisation skills;
- attention to detail;
- 'intelligent' reading skills;
- research skills;
- assessment skills;
- recording skills;
- knowledge of agencies and procedures;
- 'networking' skills.

In the next chapter, we'll continue to concentrate on organisation of the work, recording it and making contacts.

FURTHER READING

You should have a copy of, or easy access to:

• your *agency's personal information and data security policies and procedures,* and fully understand their implications in practice. This should take account of all the new media and its implications for your work. These *should have been explained during induction into your job and you should* always have access to either a hard copy or on your computer. This is a good time to re-read these.

• Your agency is also likely to provide proformas and guidance on report preparation. Make sure that you know and understand the contents of these as they are most relevant to your situation, but do ensure that they are up-to-date.

If you don't have these or anything else you consider relevant, then you will need to seek them out, check that you understand their content and ensure that you keep them up-to-date.

Aberdeen City Council and Robert Gordon University (2010) *Professional Writing: Guidance Booklet for Social Work Practitioners* (Second edition) is an excellent document which offers an intelligent and clearly written perspective on the whole area of report writing. Available to download at **http://data. learningnetworks.org.uk/news/332/Professional_Writing_Guidance_Booklet_edition_2.pdf.**

www.ico.gov.uk provides useful information for both the general public and organisations about the law on data protection and personal information.

Courses and visits

Your training department or newly qualified social workers' group may provide training in writing and in report preparation. If not, discuss possibilities with your supervisor. Identify and approach staff members considered 'experts' in report writing.

If you haven't already attended a court hearing/Mental Health Tribunal/formal inter-agency case conference or any other situation relevant to reports you may have to prepare, then try to do so.

Chapter 4
Planning and timetabling

CHAPTER OBJECTIVES

In this chapter, we'll focus on the practicalities of planning and timetabling, including:

- the overall timetable for the project;

- organising your list of people or organisations you need to contact to discuss some aspect of your report into priorities;

- making appointment arrangements to talk with people involved;

- ways of making sure that you record all your work efficiently;

- confidently introducing your role to all parties.

The timetable

If you haven't already sketched out a timetable for your work, now is the time to do this. It can be as much or as little detail as you wish, whatever works best for you.

I find it helpful to use a single page for the whole timespan of the report; this enables me to keep deadlines in mind as they can be seen at a glance. No nasty shocks when I turn a diary page! More detailed comments and recording can go on running entries in the Report File.

I then divide the page into columns of weeks, which have boxes only for days on which I can be available to work on the report.

Remember to enter the different deadlines from Chapter 3 (for starting to write, completing your written draft, and so on).

PRACTITIONER COMMENT

While it may sound obvious, reports will often have their own legal or agency timescales, and the worker should find out what these are beforehand. For example, in our team, the Community Care Assessment needs to be completed in 28 days. Our team performance is monitored on this statistic so there has to be good reason if it goes over this time frame.

Prioritising contacts

In most cases, it's essential to interview the subject(s) of the report first. You can outline the areas of your enquiries when introducing the report and your role, so that they will know at once whom you will be contacting. This avoids the possibility of their finding out with whom you will communicate from a third party.

Generally, those who might require several contacts need to come highest on the list. Of course there are other considerations, for example, whether the appropriate staff member of a school you need to contact will be available after next week when the summer holidays begin.

So, the prioritised list of people to contact is in front of you and you begin working your way through it, making appointments within the near future wherever possible, and then putting them onto your plan. Of course, you'll use the same sort of planning strategies as in your normal work to ensure that your travelling time and the best availability of interview space is used as efficiently as possible.

If you have the whole time span in front of you each time you enter an appointment, you'll immediately see how it relates to the time available. Don't cross names off your list of people to contact until you've been able to enter an appointment on the timetable.

Things to consider when planning appointments

Before actually contacting people to set up interview appointments, there are some general considerations to be taken into account.

Confidentiality

You will need to explain your task clearly and this will include how you will record and use any information that you gather. Although we'll look at this more fully in Chapter 5, it would be useful to think about the issue before making phone calls to set up appointments, as you may be questioned about it at this point.

It may be best to say that you'll go into this at the beginning of your interview when you'll be able to answer questions that they may have. You could suggest that they might like to make a note of any concerns they have so that they remember to check them out when they see you.

Personal security

Your agency should have a clear policy about this and you should know that policy.

It is generally unwise to do home visits to unknown people. They may be extremely upset by what they see as the intervention of officialdom in their personal affairs. Fear, anger and misunderstanding can create a volatile situation.

It's far better, then, to arrange your first contact with someone in an agency interview room. This not only establishes the fact that this is a necessary 'official' meeting, but also will create an atmosphere in which it's easier to focus upon the task without the possibly conflicting interruption of televisions, computer games, neighbours and family pets.

Any necessary home visits can then be arranged for later when you've established the task and a working relationship with the client, and have assessed any possible personal risks. Nevertheless, you should always follow any team or office practices, such as alerting someone to the time, place and client names for your home visits. You will probably have to check-in (in person or by phone) to notify a nominated member of agency staff of your completion of the visit.

PRACTITIONER COMMENT

I would disagree with the point about not encouraging workers to visit people in their own homes – even those we have not met before – unless there is a good reason obviously. I would say that in adult care, 90 per cent of our visits are to people's homes. This gives us a good idea of what a person's environment is like and what they can/cannot do.

For instance, Mrs Jones might offer to make me a cup of tea. Normally I'd refuse but sometimes it might be useful to see if she can actually complete the task independently – especially if others have raised concerns about how she is managing alone and good evidence for your report.

Space is another issue. In our office we hardly have enough space for our own supervision, let alone trying to book rooms for service users to come and see us. I think as long as there are good lone working policies and procedures in place, and providing there are no obvious dangers, then for us adult care workers, visiting at home generally works well. Having said this, I can appreciate the potential dangers for social workers and it may be worth visiting in pairs when necessary.

Accessibility

When setting up appointments, use whatever information you have to ensure that you address the issue of accessibility. There are two main threads to this:

- the methods you choose to communicate with someone to set up a first meeting;
- the time and place you choose for that meeting.

ACTIVITY 4.1

What considerations can be made regarding the accessibility of the person to be contacted?

How might you approach these?

Why and how might these be recorded?

Comment
Considerations may include a variety of aspects, such as work, family, mental and physical health, reading ability, language, culture and so on.

ACTIVITY **4.1** (*CONT.*)

There will be clues in the information you have about the report situation; for instance, knowing that a child is enrolled at a particular school might help you to set a suitable time and venue for a meeting. Doing everything you can to increase the chances of someone keeping an appointment will hopefully take some pressure off you.

*There may also be questions of **permission**; for instance if you want to contact the employer of a report subject, it's best to ask permission of that client first.*

In many cases, the people you will want to contact will be aware someone will be assigned to prepare a report; they will be expecting your contact. However, it's always necessary to introduce yourself and your agency and your task correctly and clearly, and to encourage questions about your role. Many people, even other professionals, may have misinformed ideas about your role, purpose and powers.

Your role

Social workers need to be clear about their role in writing a report.

Before you can present your role to someone else, it's necessary to be confident about this yourself. It might sound obvious, but are you really sure that you can explain your function and powers to someone who may come to you with a whole variety of prejudices gained from their own or friends' experiences, the media or rumour?

Of course it will depend upon the recipient how much detail you give, but it's worth having a short explanation ready. This might include: some details about the report and its place in the situation; your role in that situation; and which other people you may be contacting (this should be about roles, such as teacher, family, etc., rather than about names). It's also important to be clear about who will read what you write and what information might be passed between you and other interviewees.

It's worth taking time over making this introduction as professional as possible, while ensuring that you feel comfortable as the worker you are presenting. As in all of social work, it's about you as a person using your skills and talents within the framework of professional duties, responsibilities and situations. Once you feel confident in the role and with the purpose of the report preparation, it becomes easier to deal with someone who says that they cannot make appointment times that you offer due to social activities.

ACTIVITY **4.2**

Prepare two introductions to yourself in your role in preparing a report in a particular relevant situation:

- *to the subject of a type of report you have prepared or might have to prepare;*

- *to another professional who might also have contact with the above person.*

Using the introductions you have created, if possible, enlist the help of a friend or colleague and practise presenting yourself in your report-writing role.

ACTIVITY 4.2 *(CONT.)*

Ask your friend or colleague to challenge you on different aspects of the professional presentation or more personally. For instance,

'You look very young. Do you have any children yourself?'

Do you feel comfortable in the role you are outlining?

Comment

When you explain the place of your report in the overall situation, you may also need to clarify the 'powers' of participants, including yourself. Remember that you may be the only partner in the whole procedure with whom the client has any sort of personal relationship. This does not, however, place you 'on their side' and you must try to help the client to understand your purpose and responsibilities.

When introducing yourself to another professional, it may be useful to be prepared to include an outline of how social work training prepares you for this role, for instance courses in human development. Other professionals may have had poor or little contact with social work staff in the past and you need to establish yourself in your role with them.

It is worth spending some time in becoming comfortable with a clear factual and succinct introduction as you will be able to adjust it to many situations, not just report preparation, and it will pave the way to more productive relationships.

Tips for making appointments

By telephone

The easiest way to make appointments is probably by telephone. You can quickly establish that certain days and times will never be easy for your interviewee or that they'd prefer you not to visit their home for good reasons on this occasion.

Now that mobile phones are so very widely used, it's far more likely than it was a few years ago that you'll be able to contact someone by telephone. If you've got a number for them, it's likely that they'll have given it in the expectation that someone with your role will be calling them. However, it's also true that when you phone someone now, you have no idea of their physical whereabouts, which may create other difficulties. So, it's necessary to develop a quick but clear opening to your calls. After verifying that you are talking to the right person, it may be useful to mention the report before even giving your name and agency, so your contact will know straight away what you want to discuss.

Text messages (short message service or SMS) now hold an important place in many people's lives and social workers do use them to remind clients of planned meetings. However, it's not appropriate to use them to initiate your contact with someone in the report-writing task.

You can then go on to ask if they have a few minutes to make an appointment or would they like to give you a time to call back? Phrase it so that if they are with people they don't want to know about the report, they can respond helpfully but in a way that gives nothing away to others.

For example: 'Can we talk now about making an appointment to meet, or would it be better if I telephone you back after lunch?'

Remember your call may be something they are intimidated by or have been dreading, and they may find it difficult to respond.

Conversely, you may find that your contact has too much to say rather than finding it difficult! They may be extremely upset by the situation or angry about agency intervention or even believe that you are there to solve everything. Whatever the situation, your task is to arrange to talk undisturbed when you can give full attention to their part in it all. You will try to keep them to task by emphasising that you want to make an appointment so that you can discuss it all fully.

Always send a written confirmation of your phone conversation, giving the date, day, time and place of the appointment and your contact details.

When telephoning an organisation such as a school to contact a professional, it is sometimes difficult to ascertain to whom you need to speak; it might be policy that you must speak to the Year Tutor responsible for pastoral care rather than the actual tutor or teacher with more day-to-day contact.

Telephone interviews

Some information gathering or fact verification interviews may actually take place on the phone. You may be ringing up with the aim of making an appointment to visit an institution, but find yourself involved in the very discussion you'd thought would be face-to-face. Some professionals may be happy to discuss, for instance, an unproblematic school student, by telephone. You will have to judge if this is sufficient or if what you hear would be best discussed in person.

Telephone interviews can be perfectly satisfactory, but it's even more necessary than usual to end with the proviso that you may need to check back with this contact later. It is reassuring to the other professional to learn that you will verify with them whatever you decide to write in your report.

Remember again to record full details of the conversation, using direct quotations in your notes if possible and keep this record in your Report File. Please also read the information on interview structure and content in Chapter 5.

ACTIVITY 4.3

Create two phone introductions (maybe using those from the earlier Activity), one to a professional, such as a teacher, and one to a parent of a young person before court. Think about how you will deliver these introductions: tone of voice, speed, and so on. If possible, practise them on the phone to a colleague (voices may sound a little different on the phone).

Comment
To be useful, your colleague must be prepared to offer honest comments from the perspective of a recipient of your phone introductions.

By E-mail If you've been given an e-mail address in your initial information, then it's likely that this method of contact will be appropriate. It's often the most convenient way to contact a professional, but it may be useful to attach one of those (sometimes annoying) little requests for a receipt. This method allows you briefly to put in writing your purpose and your availability for a meeting. The text of the message should be of the same level of formality as that used in a letter; don't be tempted to fall into the abbreviated forms sometimes used in e-mails.

By Post Communication by post allows you to use pro-forma letters which are provided by some agencies. If you're creating your own, try to make a letter as clear and brief as possible, and offer an appointment which is likely to be convenient given what you know of their circumstances. Also make it clear how to contact you to arrange an alternative if your appointment suggestion is impossible.

By Home Visit It's not recommended that you call at the home of an unknown or hardly known client to arrange an interview. This may display a lack of planning on your part, shows little respect for the client and may even be taken as an attempt to 'catch them out'. If you feel that unannounced visits would be appropriate, then prepare the way for this by talking with the client about it during an arranged visit, reserving your right to drop in at another time.

Whatever contact method you use to arrange meetings, it's good practice to confirm agreements in writing. It's also helpful to encourage the contact to repeat the arrangement to you so that you're clear all parties understand. It's also important that everyone knows exactly who is to be present.

Known and unknown contacts

While reports are often written on people you have never met before, there will also be requests for reports on people you already know. The first of these situations may be the easiest to deal with as your relationship with them may start with a clean slate – although you'll have to be aware that it's not always as clean as you may think!

Your interviewee may have past experiences of professionals that will influence them to be inclined to favour you or to distrust you. Prejudices may not all be on the one side, as you too may have read and heard things about your contacts. Try to keep these to one side as you verify and clarify facts and the situation with your interviewee (see Case Study 4.1).

If the report involves a family with which you already have quite a close relationship, and you are quite used to almost 'cosy' visits, it's particularly important that they understand your new purpose and task. So when you broach with them the fact that you want to make an appointment specifically to prepare the report, it's necessary to be clear that this requires an uninterrupted time with just certain people present. It is worth considering an office appointment rather than your usual home visit. This will underline the more 'official' context of the interview and show respect for the situation and people involved.

A newly qualified social worker, Sheila, was still learning about the town where she had started her first job. It was some distance from the country area where she'd grown up and also from the city where she'd trained. She'd made considerable efforts to learn about her new organisation, her duties and the facilities and resources available (and where these were deficient).

She felt she'd made a good start in settling to work in this town, and had been praised for her efforts by her supervisor who'd suggested places to visit, such as a young people's emergency residential unit and the local police team with whom they worked on some incidents of domestic abuse. Her supervisor always helped her to reflect on what she was learning about her work in this town and she was gaining confidence in her role as a qualified professional.

However, Sheila still felt that she lacked important knowledge: she didn't understand the background history and culture of the area; she didn't know the housing estates or the particular issues on each; she didn't know which families had long been clients of her team or anything of their past. While her supervisor reassured her that this would come with time and experience, and that her own different perspective and recent training were in themselves beneficial to the team, Sheila still felt that she was 'lacking' in this respect.

She was given a new piece of work to do and was pleased to see that it was a potentially positive investigation into a mental health situation. A man suffering over the years with a bi-polar condition had been readmitted to a psychiatric ward. Hospital staff had noted that he had a regular female visitor, Pam, who appeared supportive and open to discussion with the various professionals about Brian's condition and future life. A community mental health worker asked Sheila's team to investigate possibilities for Brian's future with this potential partner, who lived on a housing estate in the middle of their area.

Sheila's supervisor asked her to do a home visit, to check out Pam and her understanding of Brian and the potential accommodation and domestic situation. She was to write a brief report giving her opinions based upon her investigations about ways forward for Brian.

Sheila approached a colleague who'd worked in Pam's large housing estate for more than 25 years for advice about buses and access. Having told her the best buses and given her some tips for getting around the estate, this colleague asked who she was visiting. On hearing Pam's family name, he smiled widely and nodded.

'Should have known', he said, 'What other clan would you be asked to visit!' On learning more about the requested investigation, he advised Sheila that she'd no hope of getting anything useful from Pam. 'That family's always been trouble. All the men spend time inside; the women are more crafty, pleading childcare responsibilities to get away with shoplifting offences; kids in and out of school and in gangs. We know every one of them from when they're born onwards. Do you really think that someone from a family like that can help a mental health patient? I can show you some choice records if you want a bit of background information before you meet her.'

Sheila was able to plead the urgency of her visit to get away and left rapidly.

On her visit to Pam, she found a pleasant middle-aged widow with two adult daughters living in another area of the town with their partners and children. Pam described those families as contented, although finances were always difficult.

'Yes, they escaped this estate and even escaped my family,' she laughed. ' I helped them and I'm pleased that things have worked out so well for them. I go over there a lot and love the kids. But me, well, I'm used to things here. You can see I've got my own little nest here; my family are all around, but I decide when and how I spend time with them. They say I think I'm better than them . . . and perhaps I do!

I did escape too – my husband was in the army and we moved around a bit so I saw another side of life. After he died, I decided to come back to the place I knew best, but I'd changed my outlook and I can live the way I want; there are familiar faces all around and it's home. And now I've met Brian through my work – he used to come into the chippy where I work at weekends and we got to know each other gradually.

He's a lovely man and lives off the estate which is nice. As I've got to know him, he told me a bit about his condition. It's a shock that he's in hospital, and I've tried to understand more about it and the staff have been great. I think things could really work out with him. I'm not stupid, I know there'll be problems, but I'm prepared and he gives me a lot. We can look out for each other.'

Sheila wrote a full, clear description of Pam and her home and sensible approach to life. She was positive in her comments on the future of the relationship and suggested that it be encouraged and supported, with Pam learning more about Brian and his psychiatric condition.

Sheila had the satisfaction of hearing over the next couple of years that Brian and Pam's relationship grew stronger and that he eventually moved into her flat. Pam's knowledge and understanding enabled her to recognise symptoms of changes in Brian's condition when he could not, and they were able to avoid a readmission to the psychiatric ward.

Comment
Of course, it's not only a newly qualified worker who might encounter such difficulties. When you change role or even change your geographical area of work, there will always be colleagues who have much greater 'on the ground' understanding and you may feel somewhat intimidated by your own lack of familiarity with people and places. However, do remember that you've trained for this; you may have extra skills and knowledge, and that your fresh view may well enable a different effective approach.

Think of an occasion when you, or someone you're talking with, has 'generalised from the particular'; or when you or someone else has created and developed characters and scenarios from snippets of information. 'Chinese whispers' can occur in social work.

Comment
This could be about other agencies, or resources or colleagues as well as about clients. It might be a favourable interpretation rather than an unfavourable one. For instance, a colleague might comment:

ACTIVITY **4.4** *(CONT.)*

'It says in this newspaper that X agency is always making mistakes. But look at A and B from their local branch – they're brilliant, so the paper is talking rubbish.'

While it might make a welcome change to hear good things about an organisation, it would be unwise to allow this to lead you into unrealistic expectations. However long you have been in a particular post in a particular agency, there will always be organisations and workers about which you know little apart from colleagues' reports.

It may be useful, if you have time, to reflect upon how different an interview might be according to whether you read the file before the first meeting, or afterwards.

Key points for appointment making:

- Always keep personal safety in mind.
- Know your role.
- Practise the presentation of your role.
- Use the best possible way to make appointments.
- Think carefully about the venue and time of appointments.
- Be wary of knowledge gained in advance of meetings.
- Record even attempts to create meetings.

SELF-CARE TIP

It can be tempting to be too accommodating when making appointments. Before making contact, do be clear about what possibilities you have in your diary. Make sure that you're not going to be rushing from one interview to the next and worrying about being on time. Don't be tempted to cut back on travelling time, but programme this in. Arriving flustered and late at the second interview whilst still worrying about the first will cause more worry and may affect your concentration.

Be logical and allow yourself the necessary time to do the task well. This shows respect for yourself, your role and your interviewee.

Recording

I cannot emphasise enough how important recording is, even when just making appointments.

It can be tempting to think that because you aren't having a full-blown interview, you don't need to note that 30-second phone call when you spoke to your subject's mother and learned that her daughter was only available on the home phone between 6.30pm and 8pm in the evenings. If you're in a great hurry and making several phone calls, not necessarily all connected with this particular case, then make a quick note on the appropriate page of your diary. Using a particular coloured pen helps to keep this organised. Make a habit of transferring such notes to report and case files on a regular basis, such as at the end of the working day. This can be done very quickly and may offer you the relief of 'signing out' for that working day and being able to concentrate on your personal life. (See the Self-Care Tip on page 30.)

Recording information from these appointment setting tasks can either be on separate pages headed with the person's identity or in a running record of dates and times in the Report File.

Prompt recording is vitally important in all areas of social work, but in most report writing it is required that the author sets out the number and type of consultations carried out. In the case of a failure to contact someone, it will be necessary to be able to prove reasonable attempts to do so (for example, Recorded Delivery receipts).

The Report File will continue to be your own vital recording tool as you compile your report, but don't forget that you may also have other recording responsibilities to complete, such as case files or team records if clients are already known to the agency. Others, for example, an Emergency Duty team, may not have access to your Report File.

So, **it's always important to be aware of your responsibilities outside of the report preparation task.** During the course of this work, you may notice or be told about situations which should be reported for possible investigation. Whenever such a concern arises for you, it should be discussed with a supervisor or other responsible person, urgently if necessary.

See Chapter 2, where issues of professional boundaries and 'At Risk' situations are highlighted and examples are provided.

Keep your Report File up-to-date and attach any new information (such as assessment reports from a care facility) to the file until you have a chance to read and take any necessary notes. Keeping an organised Report File will give you confidence that you know what you're doing and are making progress. Add to the timetable as you make new appointments. Schedule in some 'desk time' to review and to decide whether new avenues are opening up to be investigated. Be aware of your need for supervision on this project and make sure this is in your timetable.

Chapter review

In this chapter, we've continued with the organisation of practical aspects of report planning and preparation, looking at creating a clear timetable with all deadlines, appointments and dedicated report time marked on a single page.

We concentrated on making the first contact with a prioritised list of people and agencies and looked at a variety of ways of doing this.

It's clear that, as a report writer, you must keep personal safety in mind and show respect for all concerned. It may be the first time that you have had to explain your job and your role in this particular task, and it's important to become confident in the professional role.

Amongst others, we've suggested the use of these social work skills:

- personal and work organisation skills;

- knowledge of communication methods;

- telephone skills;

- writing skills;

- recording skills;

- knowledge of your agency policies and procedures;

- understanding of, and confidence in, the role of professional social worker.

In Chapter 5, we'll go on to discuss interviews and how to keep them as focused as possible. Again, organisation skills will be important.

FURTHER READING

You should have a copy of, or easy access to:

- your organisation's policy on **personal** security;

- any team specific strategies on **personal** safety;

- knowledge of interview spaces and how to book them if necessary;

- any standard letters, explanatory leaflets or other materials, outlining your tasks and role;

- how the latest communication methods and social media are used in your agency.

If you don't have these and anything else you consider relevant, then you will need to seek them out, check that you understand their content and ensure that you keep them up-to-date.

Chapter 5
Interviews

CHAPTER OBJECTIVES

In this chapter, we'll look at:

- making the most of the physical space to be used;
- recording and note taking;
- directing interviews;
- introducing the report as well as yourself;
- observing intelligently;
- being prepared to deal with difficult situations.

Introduction

Preparatory organisational work will now pay off. You may have already completed one or more basic interviews when you telephoned to arrange interview appointments. As stated in the previous chapter, telephone interviews can work well and save precious time.

Most interviews will however take place in the physical presence of the interviewee. You should be able to concentrate on the job in hand; that is, learning about the situation and the people involved, and recording your information and observations in a way that will be easiest to use when you come to reach opinions and to write your report. Much of your later work on the report will depend on your efficiency at this stage, but efficiency doesn't always come easily when we're dealing with other human beings.

Be prepared

The recording of facts and observations has to be done in a way that is both comfortable to you and reliable. It depends to some extent on where the interview takes place. If it's in an office at your agency, then of course you have far more control over the setting. I find a 'shorthand' notepad is the easiest way to take notes. It's quite small and so seems less obtrusive than an A4 pad, and fits into coat pockets or handbags if necessary. Make sure you have at least two non-smudgy pens with you.

I think that a watch is invaluable unless you know there's an accurate clock in the interview venue. It's far more subtle to keep an eye on the time and your schedule by glancing at your wrist than, for instance, by consulting your mobile phone.

We've already looked at protecting confidentiality and keeping paperwork secure, in Chapter 3. These considerations will be easier to manage when interviews take place at the office. There are many reasons why this is usually the best solution for the initial interview venue, unless you agree to go to another busy professional's office to save their time or you need to assess a home environment.

Continue, as ever, to **keep your personal safety in mind**, whether the interview takes place in the office or elsewhere. A basic rule is that you position yourself with the best access to the door; it should be difficult for someone to come between you and the door, thus preventing you from leaving a threatening situation.

PRACTITIONER COMMENT

Most public meeting rooms should have panic alarms installed now and the worker can get the receptionist to show where these are before the meeting.

Arranging an office to be welcoming yet business-like

Interview and meeting rooms vary considerably from agency to agency, from office to office and in their availability at different times. You have clear aims and deadlines in preparing a report and need to be able to work in a concentrated manner. You will want a room that is available for a good length of time, and it's worth trying to ensure that you don't have to leave the room abruptly at the end of a fixed time. It's not conducive to your information gathering to be aware of the next worker waiting outside or, worse still, risk their interrupting your interview. It also makes the situation difficult for your client.

I'm not suggesting that you should plan to run over the amount of time you've allocated to this interview. However, this can be a pressurised situation for both yourself and your interviewee; you may not know your client at all and be unaware of how intimidated or antagonistic they may be, causing the interview to progress more slowly than projected.

Make sure you have enough reasonably comfortable chairs and some items which will hopefully occupy any children. Think also about your own comfort; you will need to be able to take notes easily which may mean that sitting at a desk is helpful. If it's a situation in which you feel it's off-putting to sit behind the desk, try positioning yourself to one side so that you can lean on the desk to write but it doesn't become a barrier between you and the other person (people).

Desk height tables give people something to lean on as well as being excellent for your note-taking. However they may be unavailable and too formal for your purpose. Low tables are often more useful as they provide a surface where you can place papers, tissues and so on, as well as a focus for a circle of chairs.

Home interviews

Of course, you have much less control over the environment for interviews in the home. You may have to be content with trying just to ensure a quiet enough situation, but even that may not be enough. Sometimes when a worker remarks that the television is distracting from the job in hand, the family will respond by turning off the sound. It's amazing how even the worker's eyes can be drawn to a silent screen and you find yourself trying to work out what's going on! So, insist that all televisions, computer games, and so on are switched off, or ask if there's another room available. This might lead to a much more profitable interview in a cramped but quiet kitchen, which allows the interviewees the opportunity to offer a cup of tea which might make them feel more in control.

Recording

Hopefully, you will by now have had lots of experience of making a record of different types of interviews. It's impossible to retain everything in your memory, even if you're able to rush from the interview to write down immediately what you heard and observed. And there's often something that comes up to prevent that immediate recall.

It really is necessary to take notes during the session, although initially you may feel that this distracts from the eye contact and engagement that you intend. You'll probably have adopted your own 'shorthand' from student days but if not, it's worth thinking about it now. The basic requirement is to note enough of what you're told and you see, for it to make sense later. You can then inform others of your observations accurately in an evidenced way and offer intelligent opinions and plans.

This skill continues to improve throughout your career. It may seem a minor and common one, but in this case it's a question of getting accurate, sometimes sensitive, information into a context where it may be examined under an unfriendly legal eye.

On television the police constable in court with a little black notebook is sometimes made to look unprepared and unprofessional by the aggressive barrister questioning the accuracy and the timing of that note taking! You don't want to find yourself in a similar situation.

Some social workers may occasionally use a laptop or even a desktop computer to record notes during an interview. This can be distracting for both parties unless the social worker has good 'touch typing' skills. Some have used audio recording devices, but again, replaying and transcribing require very particular skills.

PRACTITIONER COMMENT

In our team we are trialling the use of tablet computers to write the reports at the same time as interviewing the service users now. It's all to do with Personal Budgets and letting the service user see straight away how much they may get in their budget to buy services – or not! I don't like the idea of having a piece of equipment coming between me and the service user; in fact I like to write my notes up after the meeting generally, as I find it a barrier to communication so this could be a personal challenge.

Note-taking skills and tips

Many of your observations will be used to support your opinions and conclusions, but notes must be made quickly and briefly without distracting you from the prompting, questioning and reflecting back that elicit the basis of those observations.

Of course, you don't want to have your head down and be scribbling away, so you must be discriminating in what you write. It's useful to plan the areas to be covered beforehand and maybe write down the subject headings, leaving space for your comments.

- At the end of your personal introduction to yourself and to your task, it's helpful to explain what you will be writing down. Tell your interviewee that you can't rely on your memory and will be taking brief notes as you go along to ensure accuracy in representing their words. If it's the first interview then you will also need to explain that you'll want to verify dates and so on that you may already have in the paperwork.

- You can also explain that you'll pause at times to reflect back to them what you've learned so that they can confirm or correct what you're noting. This really is necessary in order for you to be as sure as possible that your notes are accurate, and will reassure the client.

- Try not to let your notepad come between you. Sitting at the side of a desk or table facing the client(s) works well for me. I have the desk to lean on to take notes but there is nothing between me and the client. I find that this helps all parties to engage with each other and thus focus on the task. This is something that is easy to experiment with in the office or even at home. Practise taking notes with only occasional glances down at your notepad. Give your client the attention and respect they deserve.

Introductions: yourself and your client

Interview skills will have been part of your training and you'll be used to practising and recording these. Hopefully the induction to your agency will have enabled you to sit in on interviews led by a colleague. You can learn a lot from such interviews and also from your own. Even if, or perhaps especially when, they didn't go the way you planned, you will have learned from needing to be responsive and flexible whatever arises. You always have to keep in mind the report framework and your deadlines, but you have to be flexible enough to allow extra time (or possibly less time), for instance, to set someone a little more at ease when you judge it to be necessary. This should pay off by allowing the client to relax and then to talk more easily.

We've already looked at preparing a full introduction to yourself, to your work generally and more particularly in this context (see the section on Your Role in Chapter 4).

At the beginning of each meeting, you should confirm at what time the session will end, as has hopefully already been arranged when setting up the interview.

Don't forget that right at the beginning of your contact is where you clarify the pronunciation and spelling of names. You can also establish the most comfortable way to address the person and how they should address you. While this point may seem obvious, if names originate from a culture other than your own, it can be important in every case.

ACTIVITY 5.1

Think about asking someone how they would like you to address them.

Reflect on your own name: what does it mean to you? How does it make you feel when someone gets it wrong?

ACTIVITY **5.1** *(CONT.)*

Comment

On being asked the first question, I've heard people give some interesting replies such as:

'Well as long as you don't call me "Mum" like that other social worker' and

'The teachers always call me Chris, but I want them to say Christine'.

This is a chance to start your relationship on a respectful basis. A name is personal and almost certainly has deep meaning for each one of us.

Introduce the report too

Once you've completed your introduction to yourself and the context of the report, you need to outline what will be included in the report. Be clear about how the report will be used and who will see it. Emphasise that it is 'private' (not usually on public view), but not 'secret' (it can usually be read by the main people it is written about). Encourage questioning about your role and the report, as a clear understanding of these will facilitate your task.

As you reach the end of these introductions, it's helpful to get the client to reflect back to you a summary of what you've said. Some people may be so eager to please you that they'll say they understand when they might not have completely grasped the issue. Checking someone's understanding of your words shows respect for the client and reflects the need to be accurate in what you report.

Some agencies provide basic written information about the work they do with people.

Here's a brief, clear and helpful example from South Yorkshire Probation Trust:

What is a pre-sentence report?

A probation officer will interview you and prepare a pre-sentence report. This may take place at court or at a probation office. The purpose of the report is to provide magistrates or judges with a detailed picture of the circumstances of your offence and your background, to help them make a decision on the most appropriate sentence.

We will ask you why you committed the offence, your feelings towards any victims and any mitigating factors. We will also look at whether there was any additional culpability, for example the extent of any violence or damage inflicted, or whether the victim was particularly vulnerable. We will also look at the risk you pose to others and your chances of re-offending. Once the report had been completed it will be presented to the court. A copy will be provided for you and your solicitor. Once the report has been presented to the court a sentence will be passed. This will either be a discharge, fine, community order or custody.

(http://www.syprobation.gov.uk/offenders/faq's)

If you can't find anything appropriate in your agency, and you are often coming across situations where you and colleagues might find this suggestion helpful, then you might consider writing your own brief introduction to, say, what a report to a Mental Health Tribunal might involve. But do check it out with your supervisor and bear in mind the comments about the differences between spoken and written word from Chapter 1.

Signposting

If, however, during the initial questioning, there are too many 'information' issues for you to tackle and they aren't directly relevant to the task, then you need to be aware of where you can suggest the person might find more information. So, for example, if you're not sure where they might go locally for information about a particular medical condition, you could suggest that you will write to them in the next week with some suggestions. Or if you know that your reception staff will be able to point them in the right direction, suggest that they call at the reception desk after they've left you.

It's important to be able to signpost the information and support facilities in the area or, if you are already aware of a gap in local provision, that you are able to offer contact details for national support services. You don't have to know everything yourself, but should be able to offer suggestions to get people started.

There are also many excellent general information leaflets available, such as *Is it Legal? A Families' Guide to the Law* (Family and Parenting Institute, 2011).

A supply of such general leaflets might free up time for the interview, but do bear in mind issues of accessibility.

Although you'll hopefully have recognised any issues about communication beforehand and have made arrangements (such as providing an interpreter for someone who finds English difficult), unexpected problems may still arise at this stage.

ACTIVITY 5.2

I was once involved in interviewing a man to whom I'd sent an appointment letter and received back a phone message to confirm it. However, when he arrived at the office, I realised that he was profoundly deaf, could not lip read and I had no sign language skills. It was impossible to find someone to help at that moment and so we had to make another appointment.

I then added some extra lines to my appointment letters, writing,

'If you have any difficulties in communicating and will need some help at the interview, please feel free to bring someone with you. Alternatively, I may be able to arrange, for example, an interpreter, if you contact me in advance to discuss your needs.'

Try to improve on the above sentences to make the offer clearer and more all embracing.

Conducting interviews

ACTIVITY 5.3

Think about the basic steps of an interview and the purpose of each step. Prepare a brief simple schedule for a report interview in your work setting.

Comment

An outline timescale is useful in order to help you to keep the interview purposeful. You may want to look again at texts from some previous training on the subject of interviewing. There are also many basic counselling texts with useful ideas and techniques for productive interviewing.

I still find it helpful to go through an old text which is practical and helps me re-examine my skills. There is always value in revisiting texts you've found useful. I use the chapter on interviewing from Priestley and McGuire (1983). This book also helpfully goes on to consider counselling skills too. (See Further Reading at the end of this chapter.)

You will choose to use the skills necessary for making the most of each particular interview. So, considering the skill of 'focusing' the interview, one person might be very anxious about the interview and display this by trying to distract both parties from the issues to be discussed. It can be difficult to keep pulling someone back to the subject and, as you only have a limited time with that person, it may be best eventually to tackle the situation directly. For instance:

> *Mr Cross, you keep telling me about your job and your home, but I feel you're avoiding my questions about the difficulties you're having with Shirley. Can you tell me about the two months that passed when she refused to speak to you? How did that start and what was it like for you?*

Your next interviewee might also be very anxious, but wants only to focus on the report preparation and is not interested in any 'social chat' designed to put them at ease. You may quickly realise that they don't want to respond to even brief comments or questions about their bus journey or the weather. Respecting this and getting on with the task may lead to a more prolonged 'chat' at the end, when the client has learned to trust you and has gained a better understanding of your role. This may serve as a *debriefing* for both of you.

Generally the 'what' of the interview will be clear to you; you know some facts need to be verified, that you need to understand the history of the situation and the interviewee's perceptions of it. These areas will be clear from the type of report and this particular situation; you will know them or will have noted particular points to remind yourself.

However, the 'how' of the interview is down to you as an individual social worker. While you'll already be skilled in focused interviews, this will be sharpened by report work. Deadlines don't usually allow for several interviews to cover the same point. You will have to find ways of coming at the same question from different angles if you aren't getting answers. You might need to help the client to identify why they aren't answering. You might need to explain again how important it is that their perceptions and feelings are expressed through your report and thus taken into account.

Reflect upon recent interviews and identify the different skills you've used both in speaking and listening, for example:

- *using open questions;*

- *reflecting back what you've been told, thus checking the client is happy with the sense that you've made of their words;*

- *in body language and eye contact.*

If you have the chance, you could arrange with a colleague to practise in a pair or in a triad (where one person acts as an observer). This could be a test run at an interview for a particular report, or could be as simple and general as trying to get your introduction to yourself and the report situation as near perfect as possible. It's always helpful to get someone else to tell you how your delivery of the carefully chosen words makes **them** *feel.*

Priestley and McGuire (1983) offer not only good advice but suggest ways of practising various interview skills.

Factual information

The introductions may take a while, but you will need to move on as planned. The next stage will probably be the verification of facts, such as names, dates, events and so on. This can lead to the client becoming impatient as they may feel that you already have this information. You should try to help them to understand that accuracy is vital and that you don't want to perpetuate any mistakes that might have been made in the past.

How you then work through the areas to be covered is up to you, but do be prepared to change your planned progression if it seems appropriate. So you may intend taking a brief life story from the person before you, but when they appear extremely anxious about the situation which has led to your being asked to prepare a report and keep returning to this, then you might decide to concentrate on this first and return to the 'history' afterwards.

Visual observations

It is not only what someone says to you that needs recording. In the report, you may also need to offer a description of how they look and live. So, make a quick note to remind yourself of anything that strikes you.

For instance, you may feel that children appear to be a bit cold and not properly dressed for the weather, or that the parents seem to have very little control over them. Always note down the facts that lead to your concern; so, in the first case, the children might be wearing jumpers rather than coats and be soaking wet due to the rain. In the second case, the children might be running around the interview room snatching toys from each other and throwing them at the wall. The parents protest feebly and then give up. It's fairer to bring up these concerns with the parents rather than just noting them without saying anything; you might learn a lot from their replies.

In the first case, you might note down 'No coats. Rain wet.' This is enough to remind you later and is support for concerns about the childcare.

In another situation, you might have noted 'old, worn-out, clean and tidy shoes and clothes', which, in writing your report, you use to support their assertion that they're very short of money but do the best they can with what they have.

In a third case, you might have noted 'hoodie', which will help you to recall a mental picture of the subject later, but is difficult to use as a simple description, with its many connotations from media use.

As these notes really are for your eyes only, it probably doesn't matter exactly what you write, but it should always be something that can later be reported as an unprejudiced description which will add to the reader's understanding of that person in this situation. We will look at this more closely in the chapter on writing the report.

Remember also to note *body language* and *voice tone and volume* when these seem as if they may be important. There's no need to overdo this as you may lose concentration; for example, finding that all members of a family always talk very loudly, just make a note to think about the 'loudness' of the interview later, without going into possible significances of this at the time.

Body language and manner will also provide clues to relationships between people; you can note how closely people sit together and how they look (or don't look) at one another.

ACTIVITY 5.5

Have a look around you; try to become generally more observant. Take brief notes about the appearance of colleagues or friends or family. Then examine what you've written. Have you noted aspects that lead to reasonable conclusions about them? Have you noted aspects that lead to immediate unreasonable conclusions?

Closing the interview

Aim to finish the task you've set on this occasion by about ten minutes before the end of the allocated time. This will allow a brief opportunity for all parties to 'wind down' and relax a little, to clarify any next stage and to make sure the interviewees have your contact details. Of course, you will also check that they have at least started to recover from any strong emotional responses that have been prompted by the interview and are aware of possible sources of support.

Report File

Now make sure your notes are safely organised in the correct position in the Report File. If possible, read them through, expanding briefly if necessary and make sure you've recorded all salient points. You will need to note pointers for future work as you don't want to lose any of this hard won information. Don't rely on your memory as this just creates more stress!

After each interview it will be helpful to reflect upon how you feel. Intense work like this may leave you drained and it's important to give yourself space to acknowledge not only this feeling, but also others. Try asking yourself (or getting a report buddy to ask you):

- *What feelings am I left with?*

- *How will I use these?*

Comment
Your feelings will probably vary considerably from situation to situation. They might be satisfaction, curiosity, frustration and so on. However, it's helpful to identify and acknowledge them so that you can move on to plan for the next stage which will build upon what has happened. This might be to note down that you're particularly pleased that your plan to occupy the small children whilst you talked about some painful issues with their mother worked well.

Please give yourself the chance to assess and maybe talk over how it's gone, so that you can move on to your next piece of work. Dealing with feelings might be as simple as recording an intriguing point in your Report File with a note on how you will follow it up.

Don't forget that even a very small break after intensive work will help you to feel more relaxed and ready for the next job. A short break could just be the walk from the interview room to your desk downstairs if you go slowly, taking some deep breaths and changing the focus of your thoughts as you go.

Difficult situations

It's impossible to anticipate all the possible difficulties you might encounter, but it's worth trying to work out in advance what you would do in some unfortunately quite common circumstances.

Difficulties may arise from the place or way that the interviewee lives. It's more common than you might think for a new visitor to be totally flummoxed by the way in which a housing estate has been named and numbered. It might have been obvious to planners that number 181 B, Robin Way, should be situated next to 4C, Blackbird Close, but you won't appreciate these idiosyncrasies when you're trying to be punctual for a first encounter.

A good torch is a useful tool even before darkness because apartment block buildings can have dark corridors. I can recall going down several paths to front doors in one street because I could not see the numbers on the doors from the road. Several doors did not even have numbers but again, I could not see this from the pavement. If you don't know an estate, you might be unaware that it boasts a Blackbird Close, a Blackbird Road, a Blackbird Way, a Blackbird Crescent and a Blackbird Avenue which cross each other intermittently. These might seem quite trivial points, but can be extremely frustrating and upset the equilibrium of the interview if you turn up late and annoyed.

You might find that, contrary to general opinion, your client is at the centre of a lively involved community where children run in and out of neighbours' homes and adults too drop in through the open door to have a chat. You will need strong tactics to obtain privacy and calm for your interview under such circumstances.

There are strong reasons for office interviews when possible as difficult situations are more likely to arise in other venues.

ACTIVITY 5.7

Have a look at the following scenarios, and think through, or discuss, what you might do if faced with these situations:

- *There's a dog behind the garden gate at the front of a house you're visiting.*

- *You're looking for an address in the dark, and you get lost amongst blocks of flats where many of the streetlights aren't working.*

- *You arrive at the correct home at the correct time and, after you get no response to your increasingly loud knocks, a neighbour comes out to investigate and, deciding that you're some kind of 'official' person, launches into a tirade against the people you've come to visit.*

Chapter review

In this chapter we've remembered personal safety and security of information. We've looked at setting up (where possible) the interview space, at introducing ourselves, the report setting and our role in that setting.

We've gone through the basic stages of an interview, and shown how these everyday social work skills come into use:

- clarity about, and comfort in, the professional role;

- creating the best possible interview space and atmosphere;

- remaining focused;

- questioning;

- reflecting back what we've heard and seen;

- purposeful note taking;

- demonstrating respect and openness.

But maybe most important is that we observe and take notice of the words, movements and feelings that we elicit, so that we can later reflect further on what they might mean.

In Chapter 6, we'll look at the actual writing process. This will include content and the ways in which that content is expressed.

Nelson-Jones, R (1988) *Practical Counselling and Helping Skills*. Second edition. London: Cassell Educational.

This is a clear text with lots of detail on ways to work on specific interview skills.

Priestley, P and McGuire, J (1983) *Learning to Help: Basic Skills Exercises*. London and New York: Tavistock/Routledge.

Rigall, S (2012) *Using Counselling Skills in Social Work*. London: Sage.

Chapter 6
Writing

In this chapter we'll look at:

- **you** as a writer;
- the timing of writing;
- organising your writing by using a framework and headings;
- prompts and tips on:
  - what to include;
  - what to leave out;
  - vocabulary;
  - grammar;
  - spelling;
  - tone and style.

Introduction

This chapter is about putting the work into its final form. All the work carried out up until now is preparation for this final organisation and expression of information and opinion. However hard and skilfully you've been working, the way in which the report is written will have the most influence on its effectiveness.

You as a writer

In Chapter 1, we looked in some detail at the power of the written word.

We've already defined our reports as being essentially *written* records and analyses, so as we go into the writing of them, we should always be aware of the possible change in status of the information and be even more careful about the accuracy of the expressions we use.

We might therefore expect to find many courses and workshops concentrating on report writing. I recently saw in a national newspaper some publicity for courses in public relations (including writing about social work for the public) and bid writing. The latter, Successful Bid Writing, was promoted as 'an essential skill in voluntary organisations'.

While I'm sure that this is true, I do think that a more basic report writing course would enable bid writers to create excellent bids as well as benefitting many other different types of report writers.

This particular course offered help in learning to write funding bids that:

- *are tailored to the funder's priorities and demonstrate your track record of success;*

- *outline what you want the money for and the benefits for your clients/community;*

- *showcase what is so different about your project compared with others;*

- *demonstrate your organisation has the skills and expertise to run the work you are applying to do;*

- *show how you will measure the outcomes of the project and evaluate your success;*

- *plan an exit strategy – or what will you do when the funder's money runs out.*

Identify and reflect on or discuss how these same principles would apply to a report commonly required in your own workplace.

Why do you think such a course is widely advertised while no (arguably more important) social work report writing training is offered?

Comment
It's worth thinking about how you are encouraged to practise and extend your own report writing skills. If there's not much training on offer, you could find out how others progress and perhaps make suggestions about training provision needs.

Writing the report

Timing

When should you start writing your report? When you first accept a report to prepare, the writing may seem the dominating part of the project, and certainly this is often how we describe the whole task. We are asked, 'Please will you *write* a report on X for situation A?' (Of course, it's not really a question and it's usually expected that we'll take it on.)

However, depending upon the type of report, we have seen that there is often an enormous amount of complex work that has to be done before the writing. In fact, the writing may just be the organised expression of an immense amount of investigation, information recording, assessment and planning. It's likely that you will be using only a fraction of the information that you accumulate and sometimes it's hard to know what to leave out.

So, writing will normally come at the end of the entire information gathering. However, if you feel that you've completed a distinct part of your enquiry and your opinion is formed from clear evidence, you may find it will save time to write that section immediately while it's still fresh in your mind. It may also be satisfying for your self-confidence In the role of professional report writer to be able to look at a couple of tightly written, clear paragraphs.

For instance, you have interviewed a family's child-minder at her home and have recorded everything you need to present on her circumstances and attitude towards the family concerned. Writing could also provide you with a constructive rest from the contacting and information gathering which can be tiring, as it's sometimes difficult to maintain a clear pathway through chaotic situations.

Before starting to write

Organise the report framework. You may have done this by the way you've organised your Report Files, but it's worth tweaking it now to make sure it really is fit for purpose.

The framework and its headings will probably be dictated by your agency and may reflect legal customs or local or national practice. As advised in the Further Reading section of Chapter 3, be sure you have any relevant pro-formas, and if none are available, copies of completed reports, preferably from a variety of writers. Even if there are no real guidelines, there will usually be common practice.

PRACTITIONER COMMENT

Looking at the style and manner of colleagues' reports may also be helpful, as is getting peer/manager support to proofread it once you have finished.

What to include

Once you have the headings, you are clear to start writing, bearing in mind the need to be sure that your style, tone and content will reflect your *respect* for the situation and the parties involved:

- All writing should proceed from a *respect for the individuals and groups* being written about.

- It also reflects a respect for, and an *understanding of, the institution* that it's being presented to.

- It means writing in a *clear simple style* that is accessible to most people. Remember that you'll have to explain the report contents to its subject(s) before the final presentation. (You may already have done this.)

- It means writing in the *'tone' used by the institution*. This may be more formal than many people are accustomed to today, but doesn't have to be complicated in its vocabulary or convey 'coded' messages.

PRACTITIONER COMMENT

*Sometimes it's important to consider what is **not** on the form and whether this is relevant. For example, I have just noticed that they have taken the Religion question off our assessment form. This is a really important question and can lead to discriminatory/oppressive practice if not asked – so even though it might not be on the form – ask it anyway!*

The accessibility of the report to all parties will be affected by your organisation, vocabulary and grammar.

Headings

It is worth looking at the headings you can keep in your own mind to ensure that you cover every necessary aspect, even when writing under different pre-imposed official headings. Official protocol may use the same headings, but require them to be presented in a different order. If you have discretion over this, then always aim for a logical progression.

You'll probably find that the following headings will cover most reports: subject, report basis, setting, history, current situation, ways forward and opinions. These are considered in detail below, with the inclusion of Report Examples and Comments to clarify the required writing style where this might be helpful.

The subject of the report: This involves current information: full names, dates of birth, addresses and, where applicable, legal carers. It might also be the place to mention court orders and any other basic information usually included by your agency at this point, such as current educational establishment and employer. I emphasise again that it's essential to verify all such items.

Setting: This establishes the context of the report, showing the intended audience and the reason for it.

Basis of the report: This may establish who you are and your qualifications (including any prior knowledge of the situation and people involved) for the task. Some reports include this information at the end, under your signature.

You will record who you have interviewed (including other professionals), showing the place of interview and some idea of the time involved in the interview. You should also note telephone and other types of contact.

This may also be the place to note contact attempts which have failed for some reason.

REPORT EXAMPLE

Here are two report paragraphs showing how this area was addressed in two different situations:

- *I made three visits to the Smith family home of about ninety minutes each. On each occasion, I was able to speak with every member of the family, both individually and together, and was made very welcome.*

- *I have not interviewed Susan's father, Joshua Peters; I left two telephone messages for him on the number provided by Susan's mother, Lucy Creed. I also sent two recorded delivery appointment letters to his last known address and also to him at his own mother's address. These were delivered but I have had no contact from him and am therefore unable to offer his views on the situation. I understand from Susan and her mother that Susan has not seen him for just over two years.*

REPORT EXAMPLE (*CONT*.)

Comment
The first of these examples clearly establishes the setting, form and atmosphere of the interviews.

The second goes into clear detail to show the different methods used to make contact and to establish the evidence for this in the form of a recorded delivery letter.

These examples may seem to contain a lot of detail for what might be considered minor points, but you must bear in mind the legal context of your work and the possibility of challenges to your report.

History: This will generally be a brief account of a person or family's life history. The more important aspects may include more detail to 'bring them to life'. This part may also include comment on events by you as report author, by the subject or by other involved people.

You will need to be quite brutal in pruning information you've gathered in this area. Whilst we've seen that old records do all need to be perused, it's probable that there's repetition and the inclusion of facts and events which are no longer relevant. You must use your professional judgement to decide what goes into your report.

REPORT EXAMPLE

'School staff say that Jo found that particular school year difficult academically; she was often late in arriving and seemed very tired. Her personal tutor, Ms Smith, saw her regularly but, although Jo appeared to appreciate the support, she said that she did not wish to discuss anything.'

Comment
These sentences were set against the background of Jo's family context during this period. The report writer has described her demeanour, the school's support and Jo's response. The school and writer don't draw conclusions here but use careful description to convey a good sense of Jo's existence at the time.

Current situation: This should generally follow logically from the history and the descriptions and cover the up-to-date circumstances and what has prompted the report. Again your comments can really add to the sense the reader gains of the situation.

This may also be the main section describing your subject(s) as they are today.

PRACTITIONER COMMENT

In our adult care assessments/reports, this covers topics such as: communication; health; mobility; personal care; family/community; mental health and memory; safety and finance.

REPORT EXAMPLE

'The regular six monthly reports, such as this one, do cause Peter and his father some anxiety, but it is to be hoped that this will lessen in the future as the home situation continues to stabilise and improve.'

Comment

Again, this sentence relies on a simple description, showing the current situation and its effect upon the clients, concluding with a projection that this will be worked through successfully.

Ways forward: This will sum up the earlier parts of the report with your breakdown and analysis of what this means.

You should also include any *assessments of risk* that you consider appropriate. By this I mean that your professional response to the situation might lead you to state your opinion about a type of risk you think should necessarily be addressed. I am not referring to any officially required risk assessments, which you will of course mention where applicable.

You'll go on to outline basic possibilities, which should lead naturally from your analysis. However, there may be practical constraints upon the situation; when explaining the options you've considered, you should also make the likelihood of their availability clear to the audience. This might involve problematic issues of resources. (See the section on Power in Chapter 2.)

Procedures for access to resources vary considerably; for instance, you may have already been able to arrange a potential placement or you may have to wait until after the presentation of the report. If it will be a case of applying later, then outline the process and the timescale for this.

You may wish to cover several alternatives, providing the reasoning behind the suggestions and their feasibility.

PRACTITIONER COMMENT

In my experience, I have found that producing quality reports when applying for funding for services is extremely important – especially if you are asking for more money than the current rates for care packages or placements. Managers want clear holistic, evidence-based reports that provide very good reasoning for the extra funding. Don't be afraid to ask for help with these types of reports and be confident in what you are asking for, as you may be asked to present it in person.

Comments and opinions: This should include not only your views but also those of other involved parties, for instance a residential worker and the subject's family.

Ask yourself what involved people think about the current situation? What do they think about the possible ways forward that you've outlined? Remember that you may need an agreement from more than one party to work positively on a potential plan.

Conclusions/Plan: This is where you positively identify a plan for future work, including more details than those given in the last two sections. It's probably also where you'll show *how the situation will be reviewed and progress marked,* and how changes will be made if necessary. This can be vital to the credibility of your proposals before a court or tribunal.

You could also show if you're using, say, an informal written contract between the worker(s) and client.

What to leave out

The above headings offer guidelines of what to put into the report. However, as already stated, it might not be so easy to decide what to leave out from your copious notes. Of course it's better initially to collect too much information rather than too little. You may take down items about the value of which you're unsure, but can't be certain that they won't be useful. However, it may then be difficult to discard pieces of information you spent a long time collecting; you might feel the need to 'show off' all that good work. Nevertheless, you must be ruthless!

Generally, everything you include in the final report:

- should add *relevant* information;

- should illustrate some aspect of the situation;

- expands on certain descriptions – statements are only helpful when the supporting evidence is included;

- should usually lead towards the conclusions you'll be drawing at the end.

REPORT EXAMPLE

'Mr Mendoza had a difficult childhood.'

On its own, this statement is unhelpful. The report needs to show clearly why the author made it: 'Mr Mendoza had a difficult childhood, moving between relatives' homes six times between the ages of five and seven years old.'

Comment

Here, while it's not necessary to itemise every move around a couple of adjacent housing estates, it is necessary to describe the disruption to his childhood and how that was caused. Moves between cities or between carers might be itemised. You will continually be making such judgements throughout this writing stage of the report.

On the other hand, there's no need to present numerous examples of behaviour which show the same thing. So, it's unnecessary to describe several incidents which demonstrate only one aspect of a relationship, for instance the conflict between two people. These can be summarised as in the case of Mr Mendoza's moves as a child.

Vocabulary

Another area where it's sometimes tempting to include too much is in the vocabulary used. In everyday speech we may repeat ourselves to add weight to our description: A child may tell you that he saw 'a great big enormous monster'; an adult that she attended 'a beautiful marvellous sublime performance by a national orchestra'.

It's usually enough to use only one adjective or adverb as a descriptive word and these should be very carefully chosen.

Vocabulary tips

Generally, the words you use should be as short and commonly used as possible. They should be understandable or be explained in your report.

Dictionary: A good dictionary is a very useful tool to keep by your side. I still prefer a paper edition, but good ones are also available online. Try to set it up so that it's always there on the screen or at least just one mouse click away.

If you fancy buying a dictionary, the *Collins Good Writing Guide* offers a page of questions to ask yourself before buying. See page 431.

Thesaurus: I find a thesaurus is another helpful tool; this is a resource providing suggestions for alternative words. The tool is available on the Internet and there's probably one within any word-processing program that you use. Alternatively you can get one in book form. It will aid you in avoiding repetition of words or phrases.

Jargon: Words and phrases such as 'institutionalised' and 'looked after child' may be understood between social work staff but are not explicit enough for a wider audience. Try not to use social work (or any other) jargon.

The same applies to acronyms and abbreviations; understanding of acronyms such as OUP for Oxford University Press (used in the Further Reading section at the end of this chapter) might be usual in academic circles, but not in general society.

Unusual terms: Words such as the name of a medical condition need brief explanations about what this is and what it means for the sufferer. Even in the case of a relatively common condition such as diabetes, there are different types, different ways of managing the condition and different impingements on the life of the patient and those around them. It's therefore helpful to explain briefly to your audience what implications the disease has in this particular case. Whilst general explanations can be useful, it's the impact on this individual or family that's relevant.

Stock phrases: On reviewing old reports, you'll probably notice certain expressions being used again and again. It may be that these really have been found to be the most effective and have been repeated for that reason. Or it may be that social workers and other professionals are operating a type of 'code'. They may use a phrase that sounds innocuous to the subject of the report but conveys something more pejorative to the court or other audience. When you're reading old records and reports, please be alert to this possibility.

PRACTITIONER COMMENT

As social workers, our profession is underpinned by values and guidelines which place a high priority on communicating clearly and openly with clients and their carers. However, there are times when a report may contain language or professional shorthand that may be incomprehensible to an outside party. Some of these forms/reports are not seen by clients or their relatives, but we still keep them on the file and use this information to make important decisions.

For example, in adult care we often ask health professionals to contribute to our reports. The medical terminology used can sometimes be indecipherable to the uninitiated (including myself!) and so you may need to get some more information about the condition or illness to find out the impact that it is having on the person.

You have your own professional role, which should not merge with that of others so that it becomes unclear who is responsible for what. Naturally you consult and discuss with others, but you should be clear about your specific role. If you use phrases which may convey different meanings to different people, this may confuse your role, and it shows a lack of respect for the client.

Descriptions: These are crucial and can be difficult to manage. Again you must guard against writing too much.

Descriptions can be simply physical, describing a person and their behaviour, a place, an institution or an organisation. They can also describe the character of a person as you (and/ or others) may assess it. This should of course arise from words or behaviour you can honestly record.

REPORT EXAMPLE

So, paragraphs on Ahmed Jones might offer three different types of description:

- *The physical appearance of the person, e.g. 'Ahmed is tall for his age, is slim and looks physically fit. He is always dressed in a clean and tidy way. He says he is fashion conscious and that he and his mother shop together for his clothes quite amicably.'*

- *Comments upon the character and manner of a person which have been displayed to the report writer, e.g. 'In interview, I found Ahmed to be a little shy initially, but always polite and with a ready smile. As we spent time together, he became more relaxed and talked more easily about his current situation.'*

- *The description of an 'institution' which is important in the subject's life, e.g. 'Ahmed attends the Lightening Project on two evenings each week and often spends the full day there on Saturdays. This is a voluntary scheme with financial support from the Council. It offers structured instruction and coaching in a variety of interests (including football, gardening and art) depending upon available finances and volunteers. Its premises are in the centre of the Glynn Estate where Ahmed lives. Staff tell me that Ahmed is 'a reliable, enthusiastic and friendly boy who participates fully'. His parents are proud of his progress there.*

REPORT EXAMPLE (*CONT.*)

Another relevant description might be a brief factual portrayal of the estate where Ahmed lives. This could include some idea of what it's like to live there; you are bringing to life Ahmed's life experiences.

Comment

The third example given here shows the use of direct quotation (by Lightening Project staff) which can be useful in reports, but should not be overdone. It can be used to show the personal perspective of a client on a particular situation, or as here, an institution's 'experience' of the subject.

Spelling

A single spelling mistake in a report may prejudice a sharp-eyed judge into thinking that this sloppy unprofessional error may reflect on your work in general. At best, it might be an amusing slip, and, at worst, it may convey a meaning totally different from that intended.

It is important to get this right and, even if you are a poor speller, there's no real excuse for mistakes. Spell checkers can be useful, but don't set them to correct automatically. They can predict wrongly, mistaking your intentions and substituting a similar word. **Always check the dictionary whenever you have the slightest doubt**.

Several reference books offer lists of commonly muddled expressions. You might for instance look at the chapter entitled 'A Guide to Difficult and Confusable Words' in *Collins Good Writing Guide* (2003), pp175–339. This offers fascinating examples, but also acts as a warning; if a reporter from *The Observer* can write, 'Here is John Major, pouring over his newspaper', then I know I too must be very careful not to muddle a couple of similar words.

If you want to work seriously on your spelling, then there are websites and books which suggest ways to do this, such as the *Collins Guide* referred to above.

SELF-CARE TIP

*An excellent way to improve your grammar, spelling and vocabulary, and to relax and enjoy yourself at the same time, is to **read**. Take a rest with your favourite best-selling novel, literary classic or magazine story. I guarantee you will extend your skills without even noticing it, and I hope you will enjoy the experience.*

Grammar tips

Grammar can be a scary issue and it can be very personal. It's best to forget it as a subject but to be aware of some general considerations and to be aware of where to check out particular points as and when they arise.

- Avoid over-long sentences and paragraphs; readers find it easier to digest smaller blocks of information. Writing guides generally suggest that sentences should be between fifteen and twenty words in length, and that some may be even less. A tip given to creative writers is to vary the sentence length; this applies equally to report writing. Differences in sentence length can add to emphasis and improve style. It can also help the reader to stay alert.

- Shorter paragraphs are easier to read and help the writer organise the information. Very short paragraphs can be used to great effect. Consider breaking down paragraphs by using bullet points. Numbering paragraphs is also very helpful to make reports more 'user friendly'. You will need to check if these possibilities are allowed by your agency's report protocol.

- Generally, use active rather than passive expressions. In some cases, however, you might consider using a passive expression which might be more tactful and less emphatic.

- Generally, use positive rather than negative expressions. As with active and passive, the different uses of these can change the tone of a sentence.

ACTIVITY **6.2**

Consider these two sentences describing the same person.

'John is a timid/shy man' and

'It seems difficult for John to talk openly and freely with people he doesn't know well.'

Do you think one or the other is better? Might both be useful in different pieces of writing?

Comment
Saying John is timid or shy implies that this is his character and he can't change. Describing his behaviour under certain circumstances offers the possibility of a different reaction under different circumstances and the possibility of change in the future. It is usually more helpful to describe observed behaviour rather than to attribute a characteristic to a person.

PRACTITIONER COMMENT

I would also stay away from subjective words like 'happy' or 'sad' as they can have a variety of interpretations. Instead I would put the person's comments in speech marks or give a more detailed description of what I have observed, such as, 'Mr Jones became tearful during our meeting'.

Tone and style

Writers need to be aware and sensitive. Try to notice how the structures used affect the tone and style. We'll look at this more carefully in the next chapter, but it is essential to follow a formal style of writing. So, the expressions you write in reports might not be the expressions that you use in speech or in a letter to a friend.

- Don't use contractions in reports. It's not acceptable to write 'doesn't'; 'can't'; 'she'll'. Use 'does not'; 'cannot'; 'she will'. As I wrote in Chapter 1, I'm not using a formal style in this book. I'm addressing you as I might in a workshop on report writing and am therefore using contractions freely, which I wouldn't do if I were writing a report on you!

- Don't use slang expressions or abbreviations. People will often argue about what is acceptable, but if you're not sure, err on the side of caution.

REPORT EXAMPLE

Don't say, 'He earned a packet working off-shore' and 'Mr S became involved in some dodgy financial deals'. Do say, 'He earned a good income working off-shore' and 'Mr S became involved in some suspect financial deals.'

Chapter review

A wide range of social work skills are used in our professional work for every chapter. This time, we've concentrated on abilities we also use regularly in many areas of our personal lives. Who hasn't been infuriated by 'official speak' and found it hard to complete administrative forms?

I hope it's clear that the *way* you write is vital to the reception of accurate information. As well as considering some of the 'mechanics' of grammar, we've also seen how these can contribute to our using an appropriate tone. Particular skills are:

- organisation of information;

- writing skills, including vocabulary, grammar and spelling;

- ability to reflect on these skills and to identify points to develop;

- ability to write as sensitively as you speak;

- understanding of, and ability to use, appropriate tone and register.

The next chapter continues on the subject of writing as we consider checks on your report, which will provide another chance to sharpen your text.

FURTHER READING

It's unlikely you'll be able to buy something specifically for this work, so I've suggested titles which I personally own; you too may have your own such books at home, on a 'reference shelf' at work or in your local library.

You'll also find many useful websites on extending your writing skills. And you can download and print guides for yourself.

Get a 'toolkit' to hand or on the computer you use for work, comprising of:

A **dictionary**, such as OUP (2011) *The Concise Oxford Dictionary: Main Edition.* Oxford: Oxford University Press. I have used an older edition of this dictionary since I was at school. I think the 100th anniversary edition suggested here will be just as useful to someone buying today.

Or **http://www.macmillandictionary.com/dictionary/british/**

A **thesaurus**, such as that modernised by Dutch, R (1966) *Roget's Thesaurus of English Words and Phrases.* Harmondsworth: Penguin Books.

Or **http://www.macmillandictionary.com/thesaurus/british/**

A **grammar reference**, such as Gee, R and Watson, C (2003) *The Usborne Guide to Better English.* London: Usborne Publishing Ltd.

The *Collins Good Writing Guide* (taken from the original Wordpower texts by Graham King) (2003) Glasgow: HarperCollins.

I use this Guide because it was given to me; there are several other similar equally good texts available.

Writing guides: Some local authorities produce their own, and you can often download these from the Internet. One helpful example is Derby's Plain English Guide, which is especially good on vocabulary:

http://www.idea.gov.uk/idk/core/page.do?pageId=8036039

Other reference websites

http://www.idea.gov.uk/idk/core/page.do?pageId=8021380

This local government Improvement and Development website has several pages on subjects such as punctuation, sentence length, etc. Its **Useful Links and Resources** section is particularly helpful. It offers several different readability tests and shows how to use them.

Mini courses in writing skills are available on the Internet; two relevant worthwhile examples are:

http://www.plainenglish.co.uk/files/reportsguide.pdf This is a short guide with exercises (and suggested answers) to report writing generally and it usefully covers many basic issues.

http://www.writeenough.org.uk/default.htm Effective Recording for Children's Services presents a well-composed guide to writing in social services. It's simply and clearly written, includes exercises and is fun to follow from start to finish or just to dip into.

Readability scores: There are several articles on the Internet about these, how to find and use them in a Word program and what they might mean. Using them to analyse a paragraph or two of your best written work might present you with some interesting insights.

http://www.ehow.com/how_4450959_article-passive-sentences-ms-word.html

Chapter 7
Checking and proofreading

Introduction

Checking and editing the report is one of the *most important stages of the work*, yet one which is often rushed or even omitted.

Checking and proofreading calls for keeping to clear deadlines for each stage, so that it can be done as thoroughly as necessary. It may be the first procedure that gets 'squashed' when time runs short, and a quick read through may take the place of a careful examination.

What next?

Once you've finally decided that the first draft of your report is complete, you can breathe a sigh of relief and congratulate yourself. You now have something to work on; you can tweak and rearrange as much as you need (or have time) to, but the basic structure and text are now in place.

It's also now in a form which you can show to your supervisor or other colleague. You've probably already discussed various different aspects, such as a specific interview, a school visit or asked for advice on which professionals you should consult. However, now you've brought everything together, assessed it all, arrived at an argued opinion and offered a plan, it will all make more sense to a consulting reader, who will be able to discuss the completed work intelligently.

I suggest that once it's finished, you take a break before undertaking your own first and thorough personal proofread. If it's been a particularly prolonged and difficult task, it would be ideal if that break could be at least overnight. But that's the 'ideal' and may not be possible.

SELF-CARE TIP

Even if time is really tight, try to switch off for fifteen minutes. A walk around the block, some fresh air, a cup of coffee, or some chat about someone else's work or about anything totally unconnected, can be refreshing. I know some people regularly use a brief relaxation technique during the day and, if you find this helpful, now might be the time to have a quick session. (If you don't already do this, why not consider it for the future?)

*The purpose is to reward yourself, to rest a little and to come back to your re-reading with a new concentration and a different way of looking at the report. Perhaps until now you've been focused on **what** to write. At this point that needs to change slightly, to **how** you've written it. This is easier if you have taken a break and can now stand back a little to re-examine your writing.*

Personal checks

I suggest at least two readings with different types of scrutiny:

Firstly, look at the more 'technical' aspects, such as grammar and spelling.

You will need to **ensure a quiet private space** for a while, in order to concentrate fully on this task. Collect together any necessary tools, such as a dictionary and a grammar book (your toolkit from the Further Reading section of Chapter 6).

Using a spellchecker can be useful for glaring errors but can also let through (or even create) some horrible mistakes. One simple horrifying example of such an error is given in a *Community Care* article on literacy of students: a Reviewing Officer and former Team Manager is quoted saying:

> *I spent 80% of my time reading reports and hours making sense of some of them. I've come across cases where parents have been sent a letter saying 'We are now going to remove the children', when it should have read, 'We are not going to remove the children'. The knock-on effect of some of these errors is horrendous.*

(Gillen, 2011)

It's helpful to let as many people as possible read your written work (while bearing in mind the issue of confidentiality). It's all too easy to miss your own silly mistakes because you're too involved in the work. Here are initial suggestions for checks.

- *Using a dictionary* may take longer, but is much more reliable.

- Sometimes administrative staff members responsible for final preparation will have become *spelling experts*. Ask around for help with grammar and spelling.

- *Reading aloud* is a good way to 'hear' grammatical errors and to verify that the report really does make sense. It can also help with punctuation, as this is intended to make written work easier to voice without running out of breath. If you find yourself gasping at the end of a sentence, you probably need to add some punctuation! Take it slowly and try to pronounce words clearly; if you struggle to pronounce a word, then check it. You'll be able to notice if something sounds a bit odd, and you might also notice expressions and phrases which don't fit the appropriate register. Assess whether the sentence or paragraph lengths aid clarity and emphasis. It's usually a case of shortening rather than lengthening them.

- A Development Editor suggests that another useful way of looking at your document is 'to have a list of final checks and then go through them one thing at a time – i.e. go through the whole thing just looking at headings; then go through again checking page numbers are all correct, etc. If you try to check everything page by page, then it's quite hard to concentrate and ensure it's all consistent'.

Secondly, check the content and tone:

- **Does the report say what you intended?** This might sound obvious, but it's all too easy to become a little muddled. For instance, you might have described an incident with two or more characters involved; anxious not to repeat names too often, you've used lots of pronouns (he, she, him, them, etc.). This can lead to confusion over who has done what to whom! A very tiny mistake, such as the wrong use (or non-use) of a comma can have very odd results! A well-known example of this is the title of a book by Lynne Truss: *Eats, Shoots & Leaves: the Zero Tolerance Approach to Punctuation*. It's taken from a joke which is quoted on Wikipedia:

    A panda walks into a café. He orders a sandwich, eats it, then draws a gun and proceeds to fire it at the other patrons.

    'Why?' asks the confused, surviving waiter amidst the carnage, as the panda makes towards the exit. The panda produces a badly punctuated wildlife manual and tosses it over his shoulder.

    'Well, I'm a panda,' he says, at the door. 'Look it up.'

    The waiter turns to the relevant entry in the manual and, sure enough, finds an explanation. 'Panda. Large black-and-white bear-like mammal, native to China. Eats, shoots and leaves.

    (http://en.wikipedia.org/wiki/Eats,_Shoots_%26_Leaves)

- **Does it make sense?** This is another aspect of the above question. I think it's useful to include both questions just to ensure that you really do catch any confusions. It's possible to become so embroiled in what to include and what to leave out, and in the necessity to describe clear evidence for your opinion, that you end up with an occasional sentence which doesn't make complete sense. Remember that the reader probably does not have your first-hand knowledge of the people and situation. Again, a break from the task should help you to look again at your writing with a more perceptive eye. And spotting this might be easier still for someone other than the author.

- **Does it reflect accurately what each person has said to you?** It can be very useful to give a sense of people you're describing by offering direct quotations from them. Do be wary about this; you must have confidence that you've captured their words exactly. Otherwise, a précis of their words will be acceptable if you can manage to read back to them what you've written. This is necessary to check for their agreement in your accuracy. Whilst this paraphrasing is an important and frequently needed social work skill, it does require lots of practice and we are not always aware of our weaknesses in this respect (see Case Study 7.1).

CASE STUDY 7.1

I remember a higher management board group holding a full afternoon consultation process. They explained their propositions to the full audience, and then asked us to break into small groups to discuss them. When we reconvened, each group had to feed back their conclusions. Of course this is a common way of structuring such a meeting and one which the management board had seen used frequently.

The 'scribe' (the person who summed up each group's findings on the ubiquitous flip chart) was a respected lawyer with a high profile locally, rather than a social work trained person, and his paraphrasing was at times quite inaccurate. In spite of his profession, he did not seem to have that skill of summing-up correctly. He did manage to condense information successfully, but in doing so, he sometimes altered its sense.

We should always at least be aware of the possibility of misinterpretation. It may be clear that you need an interpreter with someone whose English is poor, but it's not so obvious that a rather inarticulate person might require a person who knows them well to be present at interviews. Similarly they may be unable to dispute what you feed back to them. I would sometimes offer to read my report out loud to its subject if they appeared uneasy, as I knew some people would not like to admit to poor reading ability.

PRACTITIONER COMMENT

I try to encourage service users to let me know if I have mis-heard anything or written something they don't agree with in the report. Hopefully this makes the report writing (and reading) more of a positive and shared experience for them.

The worker can also be creative about how best to communicate the contents of the report to the service user. For instance, those with a visual impairment may require the report to be printed on certain paper in a certain font (or colour) and in some cases it may need to be put on CD or read aloud to the person.

- **Are descriptions simple and unbiased?** Again clarity and non-ambiguity are vital. Simplicity hopefully ensures non-ambiguity but it may sound more brutal.

REPORT EXAMPLE

A social worker had to write a brief report on a person who was hoping to start training as a foster parent. This was a preliminary interview for an exchange of information by both parties. The social worker found the report difficult to write and at one stage offered these three sentences to his report buddy for discussion:

REPORT EXAMPLE (CONT.)

1. *Mrs Biggs holds strong opinions about many subjects (such as school discipline; diet; workplace facilities) and expresses these in a very forthright manner. This can have an intimidating effect upon her listeners.*

2. *Mrs Biggs is an assertive woman who likes to express her feelings about most issues without always allowing others to contribute to a discussion.*

3. *Mrs Biggs is a brash person who does not tolerate the views of others where these differ from her own.*

ACTIVITY 7.1

Which description might you prefer to use?

Can you suggest more alternatives?

How would you feel about discussing these descriptions (and then your own) with Mrs Biggs?

- **Above all, is it honest?** When you've read it all through and have dealt with grammatical points and clarity, do you feel overall that you have been true to the subjects and to yourself? This can be a hard question to answer, but will be reflected in your confidence when you present your report.

REPORT EXAMPLE

'My initial interview with Mr Waleski was difficult for both of us; in view of the history in this case, he understandably had many reservations and even resentments against Social Services staff. It is to his credit and a testimony to his concern for his daughter that he was able to discuss his feelings and attitude openly with me and that we were then able to move on to the positive plans that are presented to the hearing today.'

Comment

This shows the reader something of the difficult process involved in preparing the report and also acts as a demonstration of Mr Waleski's strengths in working with the report writer.

In the last chapter we said that, while writing, we should keep in mind that our reports should show respect for the subject(s); understanding of institutions and systems; use the 'tone' of the commissioning institution (such as a court); and be written simply and clearly so that they will be readily understood by the majority of involved parties. These same points therefore need to be carefully assessed when checking your report.

To fully ensure that you can answer that question about honesty comfortably, I suggest that there are several, often inter-linked, areas of concern which are usefully explored: anti-discrimination; stereotyping; labelling; and jargon. Let's look at each of these in more detail.

Anti-discrimination

This must always be borne in mind. Of course, this is embedded in all your work, but it is still beneficial to examine consciously each piece of writing from this aspect. In a report, you are usually writing for an audience outside of your own organisation. Whilst you may feel you can take for granted the anti-discriminatory attitude of your colleagues, you may feel that you have to bear in mind that some other institutions are less positive. This may cause you to play down some discriminatory aspects. It's a fine line that you have to tread (see Case Study 7.2). You will have to discover for yourself what seems to be the most tactful way to express yourself without compromising your principles. Do ask for help if necessary.

CASE STUDY 7.2

In preparing a report on an Asian woman, Ananda, who suffered from very severe depression, I consulted with a Health Visitor who had been visiting her since she had moved into our area about nine months after the birth of her third child. Her husband had been extremely worried about her since the third baby and had been able to arrange a move to our town where he had extended family.

Initially, we had found Ananda to be very lethargic, uninterested in her children and barely able to manage the basic household tasks. The Health Visitor expressed her beliefs that this was due to her culture. She felt that Asian homes were unstimulating for children and that they were deprived of toys. She also believed that many young Asian women lived in a world behind closed doors, relying upon husbands and children to make whatever outside contacts had to be made.

She found it difficult to consider that Ananda might just be subject to post-natal depression and was thus unable to satisfy the demands of three young children.

I was concerned about the depth of the depression and concentrated on speeding up a psychiatric referral. The psychiatrist felt that the case was so severe that she needed a period of in-patient treatment. Ananda's two sisters-in-law arranged to care for the children whilst she was briefly hospitalised, the baby going to one family and the three- and five-year-olds going to the other. They seemed very happy in the noisy, crowded households of their cousins where their father visited twice a day. Following Ananda's discharge, the sisters-in-law continued to provide company and childcare support and Ananda blossomed as a mother. Her home was bustling and a little chaotic, but she gave the children lots of love and attention and they certainly didn't lack stimulation.

I found in considering this situation that the tasks were clear and I enjoyed working on them as Ananda and her family made such excellent progress. However, I did find it difficult to work with the Health Visitor in the face of her prejudices. In the early stages of the work, I could work on getting psychiatric care established urgently. However, as things progressed, I found my relationship with the Health Visitor became harder as she then felt that Ananda's changing state was due to her sisters-in-law's influence and to her becoming more 'westernised'.

Now this was said about a young woman who'd been born and brought up in a typically British provincial town about one hundred miles away. Her husband thanked us for helping

CASE STUDY 7.2 (CONT.)

to get 'the old Ananda' back, but the Health Visitor still insisted that culturally Asian mothers were withdrawn and provided a dull, unresponsive relationship with their children.

In writing a report for the hospital on the home circumstances, I described the difficulties Ananda had with being too depressed to interact much at all with anyone. The Health Visitor urged me to offer her explanations that this was just a rather worse case than usual of 'poor Asian parenting'.

From questioning her sisters-in-law and husband, I was able to paint a picture of the family as it used to be, with Ananda being a lively, funny young woman who delighted in dressing up her two little girls and dancing around the living room. I had the satisfaction of being able to describe the re-emergence of this agreeable young family as Ananda responded to treatment, but my challenges to this basic racist general assumption appeared ineffective.

I was unable to make any real change in the Health Visitor's attitude and it still frustrates me to think of this; they are often the only people to see what goes on behind closed doors and if they are not prepared to look at a variety of possible reasons for worrying functioning then opportunities will be missed for getting appropriate help.

ACTIVITY 7.2

Have you had any similar experiences?

What else could I have done to enable the Health Visitor to respond in a more open way?

Stereotyping

The above case shows discrimination against certain cultures and this has led to stereotyping. You need to be aware of not only your own prejudices, and those of other professionals such as the Health Visitor, but also those that might be held by your audience. There is the potential for the use of certain terminology to play into those prejudices (see Case Study 7.3).

CASE STUDY 7.3

A court report on a young offender contained these descriptions of the schoolboy's parents:

> *Mrs N. is an excellent homemaker keeping a clean and tidy house and being a good cook and baker. She 'makes do and mends' and is always in when the children return from school, providing for their emotional needs. Mr N. has worked shifts at the local bicycle factory for nearly twenty years. He provides for the family's material needs and grows vegetables for the household on his nearby allotment. Due to Mr N.'s work commitments it is his wife who provides the day-to-day discipline for the children, but she can rely on him to provide his support in the event of more serious incidents.*

CASE STUDY **7.3** *(CONT.)*

Of course, it might be argued that this paragraph shows the family in a very encouraging way and that it would almost certainly contribute to a positive outcome for the defendant.

However, two colleagues had prepared reports on the two co-defendants in the case. One was fairly neutral on the subject of family background, but the other contained the following paragraph:

Rob has had a disrupted childhood; his mother went out with his father only briefly and has not seen him since four months before Rob's birth. Since then, she has lived with four other men for differing periods. Rob says he left home after her latest partner was aggressive towards him and he moved in with his older sister four months ago. However when I visited to discuss this report, she told me he can no longer stay there due to his bad influence on her two young children.

ACTIVITY **7.3**

Consider the above Case Study; if the author of the first positive paragraph had also been writing the report on Rob and the other co-defendant, do you think they would have written it differently?

Would you write it differently?

If so, how?

Is it ever acceptable to describe clients as conforming to a stereotype in pursuit of the results you (and your client) want?

Labelling

You'll probably be aware of 'labelling' theories from your social work education; often used to explain deviance, they are also widely acknowledged in the field of education.

These have been extensively debated and form part of significant sociological works. Basically, they show that by being labelled *deviant* from the desired norms, a person might take on more strongly the attributes with which they've been labelled. This can be particularly true for young people who might be more easily influenced by the way in which they are viewed.

This may also occur with minority groups, such as mental health service users, and can give rise to stereotyping.

Nouns such as deviance, prejudice, stigma, stereotype, label, minority and their derivatives (adjectives, adverbs and so on) all relate to this basic process.

The areas of stereotype, discrimination and labelling are often confused together, and it's difficult to distinguish between them. In practice, when preparing a report, this probably isn't important as long as you recognise the serious and deep-rooted problems involved (see Case Study 7.4).

CASE STUDY 7.4

During an informal meeting of some staff in a summer language camp for rich children from all over the world, a domestic worker described the sad demeanour and depressed behaviour of a homesick Argentinean boy and said she was worried he might run away (he had access to a huge sum of pocket money and a return air ticket).

An activity leader, who hadn't met the boy, said that his withdrawn behaviour, refusal to mix with fellow students, tendency to hide from staff and picky eating sounded like Asperger's Syndrome to her. Another activity leader picked this up and they excitedly discussed this 'diagnosis' and decided it should be marked in the day's notes so that all staff were warned about his strangeness. The Director overheard this conversation, and was able to explain how serious it might be to actually write something which was pure speculation about a student they'd never even met (and that they certainly did not have the professional training to 'diagnose').

The Director stated that they were right to 'put a warning in writing so that all staff would be aware that the boy had been observed to be extremely unhappy and homesick and that there were fears he might run away'. She therefore suggested a strategy for keeping him busy and engaged by staff and had this written down and reviewed on a daily basis.

Comment

It's clear that such labelling without any knowledge of the boy was irresponsible and potentially harmful to his future. The essential aspect of planning in this case was to keep a close watch on the individual and to arrange a more formal rota of staff supervision. It's even possible that tagging him with this label might have made staff take less care; safely categorised as 'Asperger's' they might not have dealt so attentively with his worrying behaviour.

ACTIVITY 7.4

Consider the following statements:

- *Sheila, like so many young black people, is gifted with a natural sense of rhythm and she loves dancing.*

- *Football skills come naturally to Jimmy as they do to many black boys, and he has progressed through the local teams until he is now the youngest person representing his town.*

- *In contrast to most young black men, Peter is a motivated student and is determined to go to university next year after passing his A-levels.*

- *Tania is not sexually promiscuous as so many young women of her age on her estate are. She does have a regular boyfriend but only goes out with him on Saturday nights and always respects the curfews her mother sets.*

We might say that these are positive statements about the individuals involved and so are acceptable.

What do you think?

Jargon

My computer's dictionary defines jargon as firstly 'specialist language' and secondly as 'unintelligible language', which suggests that the one quickly becomes the other when presented to a different audience. You need to be very aware of this when examining your report. Its meaning should be accessible to all parties who have the right to see it.

Like most things, jargon also has its fashions. This is another reason to be aware of its use. One profession might still use a term that a second agency has left behind for a 'new, improved expression'. This is especially common where a profession does not often come into contact with the world of social work. So, for instance, a teacher may speak about (or write about) a child being in care and assume that this refers to a local authority children's home. The teacher may initially be confused by the social worker discussing the looked-after young person, who is living at her grandmother's home.

Sometimes, jargon is used to disguise the author's meaning from the subject of the report; sometimes it's used to convey a 'coded message' to other professionals. However, research shows that this may be a risky practice as shown in this extract regarding social workers reporting to Scottish Sheriff Courts:

> *Nevertheless, they do often try to communicate their moral judgements about, for example, an offender's honesty. By hints, implication and other subtleties they attempt to induce the sheriff to read between the lines of their formally neutral SERs [Social Enquiry Reports]. Such encoded messages, however, are often missed or misinterpreted. Sheriffs often do not read between the lines in the ways intended by social workers. Indeed, some techniques of subtlety can backfire and have negative unintended consequences in undermining the credibility of the social worker.*

> (Hutton *et al.*, 2008)

ACTIVITY 7.5

Have you come across what you might describe as a coded message?

Have you ever used one?

Do you think that this is honest?

Is it acceptable practice?

Consultancy

It's essential that you arrange for your report to be checked over thoroughly by a trusted person.

- This may be an automatic part of the process in your organisation: Some agencies' court departments check all reports before they are presented. Some teams have set up their own 'gate-keeping' process for reports to ensure that agreed team aims are pursued. A *report gate-keeping process* is one in which someone examines reports before their presentation, according to certain agreed criteria. This may be most effectively done where a panel meets to do this; the panel might be composed of representatives from different teams involved in report preparation. However, such systems are not intended as a training facility and exist to check that reports are fit for purpose.

- It may be your *supervisor's responsibility.*

- It may be up to you to seek out this help. If there is nothing regularly available for you, you should consider setting something up. In an emergency, you can always ask your colleague at the next desk, but for the future it would be more efficient to create a process to which you feel *entitled* and in which you trust.

Other possibilities: you can ask your supervisor even if it's not normally seen as a regular part of the role. If they can't help then they may be able to suggest other possibilities. An 'expert' in the matter of reports would be good, but you will get a lot of aid from a beginning writer too. He or she will be keen to learn and to improve skills just as you are and discussing specific reports together really will help you both.

You may be part of a new workers' group or training meetings. If so, investigate the idea of devoting a session to report preparation. This might be the place to create a 'buddy system'; pairing people up to provide mutual consultancy and support over reports.

A report buddy system is one in which workers pair up to offer mutual support via detailed critiques of reports produced and discussion of specific and more general issues raised. The evident benefits of this system can be enhanced by the pairs occasionally reporting back to a larger group. This will raise awareness of varying issues and can lead to the development of specific training.

It is not necessary for report buddies to be at the same stage of their report-writing career. An experienced writer will benefit from a newer social worker who hasn't had time to fall into a routine approach. They may bring fresh practice ideas from placements elsewhere and may be more up-to-date with research and theory.

PRACTITIONER COMMENT

I like the idea of a report buddy. I think it's a really good idea for anyone, but in particular social work students and newly qualified staff – especially if no-one oversees your work before it gets sent out.

The important issue is commitment. It's helpful to have regular meetings even if there are no reports to discuss, as well as to set up a structure for when a report request is received. So, you may agree to notify your partner as soon as you know you have to prepare a report and the presentation date. Then you could set up a series of brief meetings at a time which you've previously agreed will be most suitable for you both. Make meetings efficient and be prepared with written drafts, and other useful information. Also have the proviso that you can call the partner on the phone if you just want to get an opinion on a structural point (such as headings, or the grammar of a sentence).

What will the consultant look at?

When you have a system in place for yourself, you must be clear what is required. Clearly this will depend upon your organisation's expectations, but if these are not stated then you must help instigate the process.

Do you want your consultant to concentrate only on the content or would you appreciate observations on spelling and grammar too? How much advance warning of a required report critique will be needed?

If you become involved in a mutual consultancy, you will be called upon to show respect and to be involved in your partner's development. Of course this is only an extension of what you did on your training course and what you do with clients every day. You will also develop further in your professional role, as this exercise should involve your looking at other people's reports from the agency perspective as well as a more personal critique.

Once you and your checker are satisfied with your report, it will need to be handed on to the person responsible for its final preparation.

Whilst it is being processed, you might use the time to go through what you have written with its subject (if you haven't already done so). It's useful to take a bit of time over this as it will ease the passage of your client before the court if he or she fully understands the contents. You should know who has a right to *see* the report and who has a right to be *made aware of* some parts only.

If what you have written may be controversial for people you have written about, it's important to make sure that they understand why you have written certain things. If they are still unhappy about it, you should help them to understand how they can show their disagreement, either in person or through their representative; you might also consider making an addition to your report.

Chapter review

This chapter considers the careful checking of the completed draft, firstly by its author, and then by another person or people whose mission is to ensure that it represents the organisation's professional position and responsibilities. Hopefully there will also be checking and discussion about the assessment and writing skills of the author, which may lead to the identification of areas for further development.

Although this might seem a simple and relatively straightforward part of report preparation, it can involve the employment of social work skills at a high level.

Particularly important in this chapter are the following skills:

- effective communication with colleagues;
- assessment skills in the work of yourself and of others;
- effective involvement in the professional development of yourself and colleagues;
- representing your organisation and your professional role to the report subject;

- recognising and challenging where appropriate the prejudices of oneself, other professionals and authorities;

- understanding of the more subtle powers of communication;

- honesty with, and respect for, all parties, shown through clarity of communication.

In the following chapter, we will look at issues of presentation, concentrating on the practical aspects of preparing your report, yourself and your clients for this.

FURTHER READING

If you have time, you might look at this webpage:

http://www.forumgarden.com/forums/general-chit-chat/40959-spell-check-worst-misprint-howlers.html

Apart from offering a little light relief, it shows how some bad blunders can survive proofreading processes to arrive in public. Be careful!

When reading novels, stories and articles, examine descriptions of people to discover how they are used to convey messages about character. In a social work report, the less physical description, the better.

Chapter 8
Presentation

CHAPTER OBJECTIVES

In this chapter, we'll look at:

- getting your report as accurately and skilfully 'typed' as possible, recognising that we are working in times of support staff cutbacks;

- your personal presentation and manner, to ensure that they contribute to a positive professional image and to personal confidence;

- getting access to, and information about, the report presentation venue;

- background information you might need before you go;

- helping the subject of the report to know how to prepare themselves;

- some tips and points about speaking formally to an audience.

A well prepared and presented report will support you in your role confidence. Careful preparation is essential to your professional confidence.

The final version

Once you have actually composed and refined your report, have made the necessary alterations and have discussed it with a supervisor and/or trusted colleagues and the subject(s), it will need to be professionally 'typed'. In these days of word-processing and personal computers, 'typing' may sound an old-fashioned term, but I'll use it here to cover all methods of producing the final report.

This should be part of a set process, which you must keep to. So, for instance, if reports have to be left with clerical services five days before the final presentation date, then you must keep to this. It should of course have been worked into your deadlines, as discussed in Chapter 3. It is unfair to clerical staff to give them something at the last minute; it may lead to errors and bad will.

This scenario is the ideal; often you won't be able to do all the consultations before the report is typed.

In some situations, social workers will have to prepare the final version of their own reports. This might be a pro-forma to be completed for an institution, or it might be a longer type of report which you have to set out yourself, such as a report on the suitability of a voluntary organisation to work in partnership with your own agency. While the processes you need to follow in your preparation of the report are basically the same whatever it is, it is not your job to be an expert in word-processing.

So, again, ask for help. There are experts in every office, clerical staff whose job it is to know exactly how to do this task. Even with current word-processing tools, it's all too easy to spend a lot of time on getting some little detail just right. It's all right to be a bit pedantic about this and to want every detail to be correct, but it's not all right to feel you have to solve any word-processing issues yourself. It can, for example, be difficult to fill in a pro-forma on a computer and be able to sit back and see that overall it looks neat and well laid out. Unfortunately, a messy layout will cast some doubts on your professional well-written report.

The British Association of Social Work (BASW)'s 2012 State of Social Work survey showed 77 per cent of respondents claimed that:

> Cuts to back office support are strongly in evidence, with 77% noting reduced adminis-trative assistance over the past 12 months and 53% going as far as to state that admin-istrative overload 'could have tragic consequences' for service users as direct work . . . gets lost behind mountains of menial tasks.

> Respondents to the survey went on to report that:

> they are having to spend valuable time buying their own stamps, cleaning toilets and even hoovering their own offices because of deep cuts to administrative support.

(BASW, 2012)

If you do have to type the report for yourself, identify your problem areas and ask for a basic tutorial from an 'expert'. Write your own set of instructions which make sense to you for future use. Please don't think that you'll remember a method when you've been shown it once. I find it all too easy to forget how to line up lists or change bullet points if I haven't had to do this for some weeks.

If you are not completely satisfied with your report once it comes back from the clerical staff, then it's up to you to sort this out. If you're uncertain about how to go about it, then discuss it with your supervisor. It's important to understand how things operate in your workplace. For instance, are clerical staff accustomed to changing spelling or grammar points that they consider incorrect? Some report writers are grateful for such help and others are upset by it. As already shown, the correction of our style of writing rather than the content can be taken as a very personal criticism.

Above all, do make sure that you do re-read your beautifully typed report before you send it or go to present it. It's no good glancing through it as you wait to go into court only to discover a wrong word has been transcribed from your original taped version.

PRACTITIONER COMMENT

I agree totally – without our admin staff the place would grind to a halt. I guess workers could be encouraged to get some IT training when they first arrive, to use Word, Excel, PowerPoint, plus any in-house agency documents/reports. I think it makes you feel more confident when writing the report if you know how to use the system.

Presenting yourself

Once the report is looking beautiful and you can feel satisfied about what you are presenting, it's time to consider how **you** look. You might think that what you wear doesn't matter, because your report is sufficient unto itself. Unfortunately this is not so.

You too must look the part: professional, alert, respectful, open, attentive. And it's not only your manner and speech that will convey this; your clothes, hair care and so on will also play their part. Of course, we'd prefer not to believe that clothes can conform to stereotypes which may exist in the subconscious of those to whom you present your report. But unfortunately, they may, and you owe it to your 'role' to be aware of this possibility and to make efforts to avoid it. In their very useful chapter on 'Court Rules, Etiquette and Practical Matters', Seymour and Seymour (2011) state that you should not wear 'anything which might reinforce the stereotype of a social worker, like a flowing print skirt, long dangling earrings or open-toed sandals' (p137).

This may mean that you present your report in one of your everyday work outfits, or it may mean that you prepare yourself differently on days when you know that you are going to a court. I've heard tales of probation offices many years ago having an 'office hat' kept in a secretary's filing cabinet, to be used by any woman officer who had been called unexpectedly into court. Of course, in those days she would already have been wearing the then obligatory skirt! Later this changed to women probation officers keeping a skirt and a pair of tights in their filing cupboard. Today, they will not necessarily wear skirts but neat trousers rather than jeans, and certainly nothing too garish or revealing. In courts, it's still preferable for men to wear a jacket and tie.

Whilst the 'uniform' might be less evident today, it is still helpful if the clothes worn by the report writer suggest a serious, neat and efficient professional. Observing other personnel will provide pointers. So, for instance, if you're going to court for civil proceedings, have a look at barristers' and solicitors' clothes. If you're presenting a report to a higher management meeting in your agency, note how your higher managers usually dress for their regular meetings. You don't have to copy exactly, but it will provide guidance about the style you should aim for.

If this involves you buying (or borrowing) clothes which you might not normally wear, then do spend a few hours in them to get used to how you look and to ensure that they are comfortable. Clothes which are too tight are impractical, as you may have to spend some very long days wearing them, even travelling some distance.

Lastly, the all-important bag. It really is vital to get this right, as it displays your efficiency and organisation, and may actually affect your performance.

Don't:

- use a carrier bag stuffed with your papers;
- use anything too garish or brightly patterned (as with clothes, above);
- arrive for an afternoon session with bags of shopping.

Do:

- use a slim sober-coloured briefcase/computer bag/shopping bag. It should have a closing top, compartments for organising papers and, preferably, room for your essential personal items too;

- be prepared for security checks.

Another issue concerning clothes is that, by presenting a neat tidy professional appearance, you will reinforce your advice to clients about their own presentation. (See section on Preparing Clients later in this chapter.)

Location

Many of these points will be covered easily if you can make a preparatory visit to the place where you'll be presenting your report. Once again, I'd emphasise how this can really increase your self-confidence in yourself as a professional.

If you're travelling to another town or area, do make sure you know the full address and phone number; don't just imagine that, for instance, the Crown Court location will be obvious. Many new courts have been built over the last few years, and not everyone you ask for directions will know this. I was once directed to an imposing town centre building, only to find it filled with young children in a 'shoppers' nursery'. I then had to rush quickly to a spanking new building further out of the centre. It never looks professional to arrive bedraggled and panting from running! And not everyone can run.

Look it up on a map, get directions from colleagues who have already visited, locate car parks (and have the necessary method of payment to hand) and the station, and the routes from them to the court.

Buildings

Once inside the building, it might still take a while to find the exact place you want. So, do leave plenty of time.

One thing that will make you feel self-confident is to understand the layout of, say, a criminal court. Whilst there will be some differences due to the structure and age of a building, the essential items will remain the same in every one of them. Try to get into an unfamiliar court ahead of time, so you can locate the various areas.

Of course, the most important thing to know is where you'll have to sit, but do also note the position of other participants. You need to be aware of the main 'actors' in this particular scenario, and you need to know their function and the correct form of address to use when you speak to them.

If you're presenting your report to a meeting or tribunal, it's helpful to know if you're expected to attend throughout the whole time or just arrive to present your report and to respond to any comments and questions. Do ask beforehand what time commitment is expected of you; this will aid your personal organisation and efficiency.

Observe and be confident

Once you look the part, know where you are going and have a satisfactory report under your arm, take some time to consider your manner and how you'll present yourself. If you've managed to visit the place beforehand, watch how others sit, stand, walk and talk. Assess what makes for effective communication in the particular situation; note what you think doesn't work.

Before looking briefly at your behaviour when presenting, we'll look at your general comportment in this arena.

This may be a new or very formal setting for you. I again emphasise that preparation is key to your comfort and performance; knowledge is power in this case. You need to be fully observant and analytical about what you see and hear, and it's unhelpful to be worrying about finding the correct waiting room or where you are expected to sit. You will be able to concentrate fully if you are confident about the basic items.

A lack of confidence in your approach can also have an undermining effect upon clients or their friends and family. It might create the potential for you to be intimidated by some other officials. I don't suggest that you must know everything about the venue and the people working there, but you should have a good idea of what to expect and the confidence to know how to go about finding what to do and where to do it, if this isn't clear.

However, don't allow yourself to appear too relaxed. It's important to show your impartiality; many criminal court defendants are confused by the amicability shown between defence and prosecuting solicitors when the bench retires to consider a case. Suspicions are magnified when the social worker or probation officer who prepared the court report joins in this casual camaraderie.

Preparing clients

There will be occasions when you also feel it necessary to prepare clients for the occasion. The whole situation may be completely outside their previous experiences, and may be frightening. If you know the layout and personnel of the situation, you can describe and explain this in advance. You will have worked to enable your clients to come to an understanding of your role, but they also need to understand the roles of the other personnel and how these interact. You can do a lot to demystify the formal situation.

It is the client's responsibility to be ready for the report presentation, but they might not always understand how the process works. It is in providing this information that you can be most helpful.

You can ask them what they plan to wear, but be wary of what 'best dress/clothes' might mean. For instance, a young woman's 'best dress' might be appropriate for a night out with friends, but the skimpy top and short skirt will not impress a judge. Be prepared to ask exactly what they propose to wear. It will also reinforce the sense of the significance of the occasion to suggest that it is important to sort out clothes beforehand. Sometimes, the chaos of a family's life may be evident in their presentation.

You might suggest that whatever the client would wear to a job interview would be suitable. Many people of working age will have received some coaching in this.

Certainly it's helpful to remind people to try to look attentive and to address the right person. In criminal courts, defendants sometimes bring a group of friends to sit in the public benches. This provides a temptation to 'play to the crowd' and may have a detrimental effect upon the whole court hearing. While there is no public gallery in more common arenas for social work reports, you may still see a client glancing at, say, their parent, their lawyer or some other significant person, to see the effect their words might be having. Your role in preparing a client is not to tell them what to say, but to help them to present a simple honest account of the situation from their point of view.

Public speaking

It can be difficult to present a report and then to be questioned upon it, and fear may inhibit a good performance. As stated above, demystification and role confidence will improve the situation. If you're unfamiliar with court settings, do the suggested visits. If your only concept of a court comes from television dramas, it will be comforting to see that, say, an adoption hearing venue is very different. Most hearings that social workers attend are in simple rooms, with only a few involved people sitting at the same level around a big table.

It's likely that most of you will have faced similar situations in various situations in your life: course and job interviews, a *viva voce* on a portfolio submission, presenting a workshop to fellow students, and so on. You will have learned from these experiences and from discussions you've had before and after them.

You can ask people who are totally outside of social work for advice. Nearly everyone has had some experience of speaking in formal situations. It may be a subject that is covered at a newly qualified social workers' meeting, or you might even have the chance to attend a specific course.

ACTIVITY **8.1**

Think back to the public speaking situations which you have found most intimidating (this could be to only one person if it's a formal situation). Try to identify:

- *why it was intimidating;*

- *what you did to prepare yourself;*

- *what aspect went least well in this situation;*

- *what aspect went particularly well.*

Finally, identify what general points you learned and how this might lead to a different preparation next time.

Comment
If you have difficulty with this activity, it may be because you were so pleased to have finished the task that you immediately celebrated and put the details out of your mind!

ACTIVITY 8.1 (CONT.)

Try to think yourself back into the situation; it may help to shut your eyes and remember the sounds and smells and then your feelings may also resurrect themselves. The tiniest feelings may be helpful; for instance, remembering feeling too hot and a bit sweaty and clammy. If this is a general reaction to such pressures, then it's helpful to remember this when choosing clothes.

From this, you might draw up your personal list of simple points to bear in mind when preparing to present a report.

ACTIVITY 8.2

Consider how you would speak when describing to a friend a holiday you've found, at a good price, on which you want them to accompany you.

Then consider how you would speak if you had to address a whole office meeting about a project your team wishes to promote.

In both cases you are trying to get the 'audience' to agree to go along with your idea. Can you identify the differences in the situation and therefore in the preparation and manner you might use?

Tips for speaking during a formal presentation

Different situations call for differing behaviours, but your basic considerations in speaking will always be similar.

- **Speed:** there is a tendency to speed up with nervousness and a desire to finish the task as quickly as possible. So consciously remind yourself to slow down. Try to breathe regularly and be aware when you start speeding up. This will also give you more time to think. Don't feel you have to answer a question immediately; allow yourself a bit of reflection time if necessary.

- **Volume:** many modern buildings are built to be easy to speak in and you won't have to work too hard at projecting your voice adequately. Older official courts may present more of a challenge. When you first enter a room you don't know, assess how loudly others are speaking and how well you can hear them. Then judge how to pitch your own speech.

- **Clarity:** don't mumble; do open your mouth and pronounce each word distinctly. Clarity will improve with the right sound level and speed.

- **Do ask for help from friends and/or colleagues:** it's often easier for someone else to notice that irritating little habit that you have of stopping mid-sentence, and to help to practise to at least reduce its frequency.

Tips for body language

- **Eye contact:** in a court, you may need to make most eye contact with a judge. However, it's respectful to look around and make eye contact with others from time to time, and to include them in the process as necessary. For instance, when mentioning the subject of your report, it would be appropriate to look at that person. When referring to a welcome achievement of that person, it might be appropriate even to smile briefly at them.

  The first time that I had to give a talk to a group, I was advised to pick a person in the centre of the gathering and to direct my words as if I were speaking to that individual. However, I vividly remembered being a teenage tennis enthusiast sitting in the audience at a talk by a famous player. I felt that he stared fixedly at me and seemed to address himself personally just to me. I now can only presume that, as a nervous novice public speaker, he'd been advised to choose a person in the middle of the audience to 'talk to'. I was totally embarrassed and kept blushing and squirming in my seat and was unable to concentrate on the message! So, do share your attention around your immediate audience.

- **Body position:** standing or sitting, try to convey that you're alert and attentive; leaning very slightly forward helps. Try to be aware of what is happening all over the room, without gazing around vaguely. Listen and watch when others are speaking to you and then reply to them. **You are good at this**; you have practised your assessment and communication skills over and over again, so relax a little and speak in a considered manner.

- **Don't fiddle** with your papers, glasses or pen. Think about what you'll do with your hands. This may be hardest when sitting or standing without a table or bench in front of you to rest them on. I think it's harder to sit still, as a social worker usually does, rather than to stride up and down as a Perry Mason-type lawyer trying to persuade the jury members to accept a point of view.

- As above, **do ask colleagues and friends** if they've noticed any fidgety or distracting habits you might have. On questioning, they may realise that you have the ability to irritate without realising it, by small gestures you habitually make.

Content

Of course the substance of what you say is the most important aspect. If you feel the questioner is trying to make you say something different from what you believe, you can always refer back to what you've written:

> *As I say in my report, I think that . . .*

This is a version of the 'broken record' technique which you may have learned on, for instance, an assertiveness course.

Try not to be swayed from what you believe. Your assessment and the resulting conclusions are the result of careful professional work and fulfil your remit. Others may have different interests in the situation. Unless some new information emerges during the process, there should be no reason for you to change your view. Even if some important new information is introduced, it might be more appropriate to ask for time to consider it, and discuss it with the subject, than to change your opinions without reflection.

You are not the only one . . .

It may give you more confidence as you go into presenting to remember that you are not alone. Nearly every person present in a court (or tribunal, or conference, and so on) will have some unease about speaking in this arena.

We saw in Chapter 1 how judges *chose* to follow refresher courses in the craft of judging; they were prepared possibly to expose their weaknesses in front of fellow judges in order to improve their work. And, of course, they realised that they would learn by watching their peers practising in this way. There is always room for improvement in every profession, and the wisest participants know this and are constantly observing others to gain tips on how (or how not) to present themselves.

Traditionally, social workers have learned the practice of their profession by 'shadowing' more experienced workers. Sometimes the most helpful approach that these role models can give is to explain their own vulnerability in the report preparation and presentation process; to show that it is usual to feel nervous, but that confidence will grow as thoughtful and thorough preparation leads to satisfactory performance.

Chapter review

We've looked at various aspects of the report writer's presentation, including tips for speaking in public.

Professional role confidence is improved when you know where you have to go and what you have to do. You may also feel that this confidence will stand you in good stead with the other professionals who are present.

Social work skills you will particularly need to call on will be:

- working with clerical/administrative/support staff;
- self-presentation;
- self-awareness and understanding of the necessity to adapt your approach according to the audience;
- effective communication with individuals;
- addressing groups;
- inter-professional interaction;
- understanding of, and comfort in, the professional role.

The final chapter will consider the aftermath of the report submission (feelings, changes, organisation and so on), what you've learned from the experience and any future work.

Rozenberg, J (8 February 2012) 'Wigs off, jeans on at the Judicial College'. **www.guardian.co.uk**

Seymour, C and Seymour, R (2011) *Courtroom and Report Writing Skills for Social Workers*. Second edition. Exeter: Learning Matters.

Chapter 9
And afterwards?

CHAPTER OBJECTIVES

In this chapter, we'll look at:

- the 'results' of your work;

- the particular difficulties of a waiting period for these;

- the immediate emotional and practical impacts upon the people involved;

- the immediate emotional and practical impacts upon you, the report author;

- practical aspects (what do you do with your Report File and other papers?);

- implications for the future with the need to consider change, endings and beginnings;

- reflection on the whole process and identification of your professional developmental needs.

This chapter is about tidying up and moving on. The completion of a report can be a time of heightened emotions and feelings for all parties (including social workers) and this should be taken into account throughout the chapter.

Results

As the report writer, you will naturally be keen to know the outcome of all your efforts. Sometimes, there's not much doubt about this, but on other occasions you may not be so sure. The waiting period can be particularly difficult where there is an adversarial atmosphere. And, occasionally, the report writer can be caught up in that conflict. For instance, parental disputes over residence and contact may result in two parties each trying to impress the writer while denigrating the other. If someone feels the report writer has favoured the other side then that party may feel aggrieved and blaming. Such attitudes can arise even where the writer has been scrupulously fair; after all, it's someone's family and parenting skills that are being called into question. Feelings may be set from years of bitter conflict.

So the final presentation of the report may not be achieved with a sigh of relief. You should always be prepared for fall-out even if you cannot imagine where it might come from. If you anticipate serious difficulties, you should consider having a colleague with you for support. Your supervisor may well suggest accompanying you, but even if you're well used to report preparation, you should still consider asking for support in a possibly problematic situation.

It is sometimes surprising that it's at this stage that your clients show that they haven't completely understood the reality of the situation. You know that you've done everything possible to alert them to the possible outcomes, but when results are actually announced, they may seem shocked or not to understand the practical implications of what has happened. If this occurs, try not to blame yourself (or to let them blame you), but concentrate on dealing with the practicalities. Do whatever has to be done to move the situation on. This might be something like fetching someone's belongings or making an arrangement about when and where people will meet again. Hopefully, even if the result is upsetting, it will be the start of a planned progression along a path towards the best possible situation under the circumstances.

Emotions often spill out at the end of a report process. This isn't surprising when you consider the tensions that have built up. Even a straightforward expected outcome can produce tears or screams of delight or even aggression between two parties. If someone feels they have no more to lose, then they may suddenly feel freed to behave angrily.

So do be prepared for a very emotional time. And please don't forget yourself; you have been working under the pressure of conflicting demands and expectations. While you may have an official debriefing planned for later, have you thought about what you will do as you walk away from this situation? Of course you may be involved in some very practical tasks, such as taking someone to a residence some distance away, but there will be a time when this situation is completed – at least for today – and you have to wind down.

SELF-CARE TIP

I suggest you create a short list of possible tension releases/relaxers/brief instant pleasures to be used at times like these. Take a few minutes to create such a list and keep it stuck on your noticeboard or in the front of your diary or even in a small plastic photo frame on your desk. It can be anything realistic you fancy: a quick trip to the tea shop down the road, a walk in the park, a trip to the top of your office block where you can look out over the surrounding area . . .

Practical organisation

What happens now to your carefully maintained and invaluable Report File?

There will be organisation rules about some official papers and you should know these. Remember that your agency has legal responsibilities for making sure that some official administrative papers are sent or filed in the correct manner. This might not be your personal responsibility, but you must be sure that you've handed over everything required to the appropriate person.

No doubt you will have lots of other notes, papers and pieces of information which you've gleaned along the way. You will have used these in writing your report, or will have decided not to include them. You may have given some of this additional information to another organisation, such as a new residential situation.

Whatever use has been made or not made of your notes, they should not be kept. If there is any further information you anticipate will be useful, then record it briefly in your official records. All notes referring to the report should be shredded or supplied to your official confidential waste disposal system. You will know the system for your particular office. Please make sure that any old files or reports are returned and that your Report File is empty at the end of the whole process. This should be beneficial to your peace of mind as it creates a clean line under the report. Any further work you might undertake with the situation will be under a different role or piece of work.

This piece of clearing-up should be done very soon after the conclusion. Social workers may be 'hoarders' at work as well as at home!

It may be useful to involve the subject of the report in some parts of this process; see under Comment below Activity 9.1.

Change and the social work relationship

This stage may be the beginning of a long-term plan in which you, as the report writer, are centrally implicated; or, quite simply, you may never see these people again. Even where the report has just been one event in a long relationship between you and this particular client, it is likely that completing the process will have changed that relationship.

Ending a social work relationship

Of course, this may be the end of an intense piece of work. The client may no longer be involved with a social worker and may have become quite dependent upon you during the process. In this case, you will need to draw on your skills in ending social work relationships. Be sure that you know what resources are available for the client in case of need, and make sure that you communicate how and where these are to be found. It's probably not appropriate to hand over leaflets as you leave a court or to name useful organisations at this stage. Either arrange for a concluding interview or agree to send information by post, so that the client has time to absorb and reflect upon what's happened. They will then be ready to concentrate on possibilities for the change.

If the situation means that the client will now be working with someone other than you, arrange appropriate transfer arrangements. Think about how this change will be effected to create a positive way forward. Working with someone through an intense period of his or her life allows a strong relationship to develop and you will need to make an effort to enable the client to feel strong about moving on.

Again, don't forget yourself and your feelings of attachment to the client in this situation.

ACTIVITY 9.1

Consider working with endings. You may wish to think back to other times when you've worked with concluding a social work relationship or where you've taken over from someone closing a relationship.

What elements do you think might help to enable the client to move on positively? What can you try to put in place to enable a useful new path forward under different circumstances?

ACTIVITY 9.1 (CONT.)

Comment

It can be helpful to tie in your recording and your practical work to show your client that all your activities are part of a whole social work relationship. So, this process might be a 'tidying and tying up' of several aspects. If you have to write a concluding or transfer record summary, this can be constructed together with the client, so that they know and contribute to what is passed on or left to lie on a closed record. You can show how you destroy the notes you've taken whilst preparing the report and what will happen to any written records of the whole process.

Opening a social work relationship

Sometimes the report completion will mark the start of your task; you might be the main worker involved in the carrying out of the agreed plan. In an ideal world, you'd already have been introduced as such and the client would have started to get to know you. However, social workers' time constraints may mean this isn't possible.

ACTIVITY 9.2

Although you may not have been involved in the report preparation, it may result in an important piece of work for you. Would you approach meeting a new client from this source (i.e. someone with whom you are starting a social work relationship as a result of a written plan or report compiled by another worker) in a different way from usual? How much would you refer back to their recent report experience?

Comment

Even when you haven't been involved in the preparation of a report, the process of its preparation might be very important to your future work with a client. If the client hasn't been enabled to understand the procedure and the roles of different people, then misunderstandings may persist which can hamper progress.

It's therefore important to commence by helping the client to express their understanding of the whole process and how they see their current situation. You might be surprised to learn that their concept of the proceedings is not the same as that of the involved professionals. Don't forget that they may have been under considerable emotional pressures which can easily distract and distort perceptions.

One way to approach the new status is to show it as a new beginning; the client has a history which is recorded in the report, but now there is the possibility of a new start. Even if the future holds a continuation upon a path which has already been started, this is still a point at which understanding and attitudes can alter and lead to an enhanced progression.

This is true of the social worker as well as of the client. So, if you are the newly involved social worker after the report, you are not necessarily constrained by the report writers' perceptions.

For instance, the writer might have had doubts about the client's persistence in working on the defined plans. However, on meeting the person and asking them how they see the current situation and the future, you might realise that their reluctance over some details arises from an insecurity about their ability to manage some administrative aspects. You then find that your offer to accompany them to manage the first of these, and help in learning to manage for themselves, resolves these issues. It's important that you take the time to assess or reassess your own perceptions of the person and the situation.

Changing a social work relationship

With the different priorities and roles involved in report preparation, you might both have come to see each other in a slightly different light. Officially it might be a new beginning to that professional relationship (new orders, new home, and so on), but even if not, it's a useful time to call a halt and reassess what has happened and where you plan to go from here. This can have a very positive effect on your social work. It may be an appropriate time for all parties to put in some extra work to achieve a goal, or it might be an appropriate time for the social worker to start to relax their efforts and to allow the client to move on more independently.

The main aspect for many participants in the process will be changing contacts and relationships. While this might be clear in, for example, a client moving on to a new residential facility or gaining a new worker to concentrate on a specific need (such as improving their literacy or finding suitable training opportunities), it may not be so easy where an existing relationship will change.

This might be a change in the relationship with the social worker (possibly you); for instance, a client moving into a drug rehabilitation scheme might have a change in their 'key worker'. Previously it was the social worker in the field but, for the foreseeable future, it becomes someone on the spot in the residential facility. This may require the field social worker to take a back seat and to be less immediately involved, at least for a while.

This can be hard to accept and you may need to discuss your feelings and perceptions with a supervisor or colleague.

Depending upon the situation and the protocol in your office, you might be the designated 'Case Manager' in circumstances where, for the immediate future, you will have little direct work with the client. This may bring in the need to extend your management skills, as you may be coordinating, overseeing and consulting on a range of issues.

Whatever the different aspects of each case, do make the most of the 'new start' opportunities in every scenario. Even where everything might look set to continue exactly as before, the client and you will have changed at least slightly. You may be able to discuss together how your reactions and attitudes have altered and how this might affect future progress.

For example, if you've noticed that your client has become less defensive when asked about their parents, you could mention this and tell them how you've found that this makes your monthly interview with them more profitable. This demonstrates an evolving relationship and shows how change can benefit the social work relationship.

Learning and professional development

Every piece of social work is an opportunity to learn and develop. Once the whole process is completed and any resulting work has started, you will benefit from an assessment of the whole report procedure.

The report as a document

I have known some regular report writers who created their own personal performance assessment sheet which they used after each report. We might not all have the chance to do this but if you can make time, try to make a brief list of points to look at each time, with the addition of extra questions which you feel are especially pertinent to a particular report.

Points/questions might include items such as:

- Does it read well?

- Do you think the 'characters' are fairly and clearly described?

You will find ideas for pertinent points in Chapter 7: Checking and Proofreading, and it should be simple to draw up a list using topics covered there. However, this needs to be a relatively brief task, so keep your list short or the temptation will be to put it off until you have more time.

This exercise can usefully be done:

- with a supervisor;

- with a report buddy;

- with a report panel, who may also perform this task;

- alone, if there's is no one else available. Although it's always beneficial to have another critical eye examining your report, even working alone you'll still find some useful learning points about your development.

Social work report skills

After looking at the report as a document, you can go on to assess your skills shown in working on the task. Again, it will depend upon the type of report and your role, but it will be helpful to think about your management of each part of the task:

- your organisation and planning of the task;

- your interviews: creating constructive atmosphere, structure, getting information and so on;

- your recording of information as you go along;

- your assessment of the situation and planning the best possible realistic outcome;

- your knowledge of your agency and resources;

- your organisation of knowledge to write a relevant succinct report, which clearly expresses your opinions about the situation.

These points (and any others you've added as important to you) should encourage a re-examination of the social work skills you've used. It should therefore enable you to note which ones you particularly want to work on (see Case Study 9.1). The timescale and deadlines create pressure, so that you may feel you didn't have enough time to cover certain aspects as fully as you would have liked. However, we do have to work within a set structure and this cannot always be changed for the sake of individuals.

CASE STUDY **9.1**

A social worker, Jan, had to prepare court reports on three young offenders for the Youth Justice Court. Although these young people had committed the same offence together, attended the same school and lived on the same estate, it was much harder to get information about the offender from one family than from the other two. Jan felt that she had not got to the bottom of the situation by the time that she had to write her report. However, it's only possible to ask for more time if you have a very serious reason to do so, and this was not one. She showed that she wasn't entirely satisfied with her enquiry by including the following statement in her report:

> *'Despite two lengthy interviews with Peter and his parents, Mr and Mrs Brenner, and a further interview with Peter alone, I am still not sure what prompted his involvement in these offences. Peter is a quiet boy and repeatedly told me that he had "no idea" why he became involved. He does not usually spend time with the other two defendants either inside or outside school. This is confirmed by the observations of school staff and his parents.'*

The process cannot allow for an individualised approach. The length of time allowed for reporting on all three defendants should be the same. So if dissatisfaction arises from some such issue, you must acknowledge to yourself that you have to work within these constraints and that that is one reason why report preparation can be such a challenging piece of work.

So following the completion of this report preparation task, social worker Jan noted her dissatisfaction with this aspect and re-examined her approach. She felt that she needed more practice in effective interviewing. In this example of Peter Brenner, she considered the way she had structured the interviews: might it have worked better if she'd spent more time alone with Peter gaining his confidence?

Would it have been helpful to meet with each parent separately as well as together, and to have also seen them without Peter?

In discussion with her supervisor, Jan came to understand that family interviews can be very hard for a single worker. In this example she might have felt that the three family members were presenting a united front against her and were determined not to say what had happened (although, of course, it's also quite possible that they really couldn't explain Peter's involvement in the offending). However, it's not easy to conduct and direct a meeting in such a case.

It can be equally hard to keep moving forward and to get information when there's a rift between parties. In the case of young offenders, it's not unusual to find in a family interview

---

that they refuse to speak to their parents and only answer your questions by 'yes', 'no' and 'don't know'; or you may have to deal with aggressive outbursts between parties.

There is a definite case for co-working interviews with more than one participant, and Jan was encouraged to look at possibilities for future reports.

In this example the report author was able to pinpoint an area in which more practice is needed, such as conducting family/group interviews, and she noted this and later consulted social work texts on the subject, enquired about training possibilities and generally asked colleagues what they had found helpful.

However, she also realised that she done the best possible report under the constraints of the task, and that afterwards she had to move on to working on gaining experience.

I'd again emphasise that you cannot be perfect at any social work task. You are dealing with complex human interactions (and this includes your own involvement), and every situation is dynamic. You might decide after a certain experience that you would do something differently next time, but when you come to put this into practice, you might find that your first approach would actually be more useful in this new situation.

When assessing your performance, do remember to ask not only what went well or not so well but also *why.* This is key to improving weaker areas and to making concentrated use of strong areas. Hindsight is not only also useful in thinking constructively about how you might have improved your effectiveness in some way, but also in demonstrating that sometimes there is nothing you could have done differently to get better results.

Wider issues

You can also assess your report from the viewpoint of some of the wider issues which were raised in Chapter 2 on General Considerations. You may like to consider how your report and enquiries might influence agency or local political policy.

We looked at the subject of change earlier in this chapter and this word figures in many definitions of social work; an example is that of the International Federation of Social Work:

Professional social work is focused on problem solving and change. As such, social workers are change agents in society and in the lives of the individuals, families and communities they serve.

(http://ifsw.org/policies/definition-of-social-work, 8 June 2012)

You can consider the report scenario from this angle: how has the function of change agent been brought into play?

New light on your professional role

Reporting to courts, tribunals, case conferences and so on might be fairly common for you, and you have become used to your role there. However, there's always the possibility that other professionals see your role in another light and you will always need to maintain your awareness of this. Do remember that different venues will have different personnel and may have slightly different procedures. One solicitor may have a contrasting approach to social workers from another, and one clerk may have a slightly different concept of the power of a social worker from another.

So, when you've experienced one or more of these report situations, be prepared to assess yourself again in your professional role. This might be useful as a part of formal supervision, but if it doesn't happen, you could possibly find help in ongoing professional development training, a new workers' support group or just by sharing report presentation experiences with another worker. In such a concentrated piece of work, it's most important to reflect upon what's happened and the differences of others' perceptions of social workers in that particular arena. It's most useful if you can do this very soon after the event, so that the impact of your feelings remains.

ACTIVITY 9.3

Can you think of (or if not, have you been told about) a situation in which a social worker was praised in a court or similar place? What was the role of the person praising and what did they comment on favourably?

And now think of a situation (or one you've been told about), in which a social worker received a less favourable assessment from another 'actor' in the scenario. Again, who was it and what did they say?

In both examples, say if you think the comments were justified. Did they apply to this particular social worker in this particular case or were they offering a more general opinion? For instance a judge might say 'Thank you to Mr Barker for his very helpful report, which is something I've come to expect from his department'.

How do these comments make you feel about your professional role?

Do you feel 'responsible' for how your profession is regarded?

Finally, you might think about what, if any, are the differences between your everyday professional role and your report writing professional role?

Chapter review

In this chapter I've looked at what might seem the deflating process of the end of the work. Tensions and pressures of time constraints and the acknowledgement of the vital importance of the process can lead to stress and anxiety in all parties. We've seen that it's necessary to plan how to deal with these reactions.

We've also considered reflecting and acting upon your previous learning and experience of working in situations of change, of endings and of beginnings.

As in most of the chapters, you have also been advised to look at your personal organisation and your performance in the professional role.

The main social work skills required at this stage are:

- social work with changes;

- drawing the social work relationship to a conclusion;

- opening new social work relationships;

- reflection on and assessment of work done;

- recognition of learning achieved;

- recognition of necessary future learning and professional development.

You have already learned (and hopefully practised) all these skills, but we always need to continue to develop. No two pieces of social work can ever be exactly the same; we should take this fact as a wonderful opportunity to learn something from each new experience.

Congratulate yourself on a job done as well as possible and on identifying some ways of constructively moving forward in your professional development.

FURTHER READING

Trevithick, P (2012) *Social Work Skills and Knowledge*. Third edition. Maidenhead: Open University Press.

This aids the reader in considering all aspects of change from the developmental to the very practical aspects of changing contacts. See, in particular, Chapter 5: Understanding Human Beings (pp124–49) and Chapter 7: Interviewing Skills (pp219–49).

Afterword

I hope that this book is useful to you and fulfils my intentions of providing a practical aid set against a background of social work theory and our society today. I hope also to have encouraged critical reflection in many directions, but perhaps most importantly, a renewed enthusiasm to accept the constant challenges and consequent need to develop throughout the social work career.

It's fruitful to look at official bodies' standards and compare your progress against their descriptions of required skills and their development. I suggest reminding yourself from time to time of the 2012 mapping of the Health and Care Professions Council (HCPC)'s Standards of Proficiency (SOP) for social workers in England against the Professional Capabilities Framework (PCF). This is available at: **http://www.hpc-uk.org/assets/documents/10003B0BMappingoftheHPC'sstandardsofproficiencyforsocialworkers-inEnglandagainstthePCF.pdf**

The College of Social Work also provides a mapping tool, with a link to this at: **http://www.collegeofsocialwork.org/**

> *The HPC standards of proficiency are the threshold standards necessary for safe and effective practice within a profession. They set out what a social worker in England must know, understand and be able to do following the completion of their social work degree.*

> *. . . By contrast, the PCF is designed to support social workers throughout each stage of their career, beyond the threshold standards set by the HPC.*

> *The PCF acts as an overarching framework by setting out key capabilities expected of a social worker as they develop in their career. These include professionalism, values and ethics, knowledge, intervention and skills and professional leadership.*

> **(http://www.collegeofsocialwork.org/pressrelease.aspx?id=6442451341**, 2012)

I'd like to make suggestions for two ways of functioning that may be helpful to your progress through the skill development referred to in the above documents. These aren't new and I'm sure most of you already follow them, but you might be able to do so more consciously and critically.

The first is to be open to learning about and understanding what is going on around you; in this I include events and developments in family, friends, work and community, and also changes and happenings in the wider world.

We are fortunate to live at a time when information is usually quickly accessible via the Internet. The Internet not only allows us to keep up with research, legislation, new medical treatments, public reports and reviews and so on, but also with events and changes in the social and political arenas.

This morning I saw a link 'Could Social Workers have prevented toddler's death?' on *The Guardian*'s Society Briefing, which led me to The Children's Services Blog on the Community Care website. This provided a brief account of this subject with links to other 'angles', and I was very quickly able to consult the Serious Case Review.

However, this involved trusted sites and we should never forget that almost anyone can post almost anything. On the same visit to the Community Care site, I learned that:

> Councils across Britain and Cafcass are considering taking legal action against a . . . site that has named and pictured social workers whom they employ.

> The news follows a successful campaign by social workers to have the site's related Facebook page taken down.

> The website names and pictures over 20 social workers and other child protection professionals alongside Nazi imagery. It is run by a campaign that seeks to expose professionals for the supposedly unjust removal of children through care proceedings.

(Samuel, 2012)

Hopefully this will be where the positive aspects of our society's laws will come into play.

So, this morning I extended my knowledge and understanding of the world of social work in 30 minutes spent at my desk. Hopefully I will be able to enjoy debating them with people I meet in the next few days.

I do feel privileged that today there are individuals and organisations out there alerting me to what is going on. The downside is being distracted from work by following fascinating trails of information. I combat this by allowing only a certain amount of time each morning to consider the 'news' and I don't oversubscribe to e-mail feeds. We must be organised as well as receptive!

The second area I wish to emphasise is that of self-care. This should become a conscious process and not just one to which you pay lip-service.

We are good at caring for others, but not necessarily for ourselves. The tips throughout this book aren't new or complicated. What you do to look after yourself may be very different from what I'd do, and our circumstances may be different, but I'd ask you make a conscious effort to bring this aspect of living to mind on a regular basis.

The easiest way to do this is to tie it in with certain simple stages. For instance, your interviews usually take place on the fourth floor of an office block and you walk downstairs to your writing desk on the second floor; pausing to look out of the window on the third floor while doing some deep breathing will mark the end of one activity and re-energise you for the next. This simple process will come to mind every time you make that short journey!

I hope these suggestions will help you develop positive habits to benefit you in both your professional and your personal life as an effective social worker.

Bibliography

Aberdeen City Council and Robert Gordon University (2010) *Professional Writing: Guidance Booklet for Social Work Practitioners.* Second edition. Aberdeen: Aberdeen City Council.

BASW (2012) The State of Social Work. *Professional Social Work*, May. Available at: **http://cdn.basw. co.uk/upload/basw_23651-3.pdf**

Bottoms, A and Stelman, A (1988) *Social Enquiry Reports.* Aldershot: Wildwood House.

Collins Good Writing Guide (taken from the original Wordpower texts by Graham King) (2003). Glasgow: HarperCollins.

Dominelli, L (2008) *Anti-Racist Social Work.* Third edition. Basingstoke: Palgrave Macmillan.

Dutch, R (modernised by) (1966) *Roget's Thesaurus of English Words and Phrases.* Harmondsworth: Penguin Books.

England, H (1986) *Social Work as Art.* London: Allen & Unwin.

Family and Parenting Institute (2011) *Is It Legal? A Families' Guide to the Law.* Fourth edition. Available at: **www.familyandparenting.org**

Gee, R and Watson, C (2003) *The Usborne Guide to Better English.* London: Usborne Publishing Ltd.

General Social Care Council (2011) *Professional Boundaries: Guidance for social workers.* London: GSCC.

Gillen, S (2011) 'Improving social workers' literacy'. *Community Care*, 5 September. Available at: **www. communitycare.co.uk**

Grace, M (2002) Power of the written word. *British Dental Journal*, 193(11): 607.

Guilfoyle, M (2012) Book review: *Probation and Social Work on Trial. Probation Journal*, 59(1): 81–3.

Health and Care Professions Council (2012) *The Standards of Proficiency.* Available at: **www.hpc-uk.org/ assets/documents/10003B08Standardsofproficiency-SocialworkersinEngland.pdf**

Hopkins, G (1998) *Plain English for Social Services.* Lyme Regis: Russell House Publishing.

Howe, D (2009) *A Brief Introduction to Social Work Theory.* Basingstoke: Palgrave Macmillan.

Hutton, N, Halliday, S, McNeil, F and Tata, C (2008) *Social Enquiry Reports and Sentencing in Sheriff Courts: Full Research Report ESRC End of Award Report, R000239939.* Swindon: ESRC.

Jones, R (2009) 'In praise of the Social Work Taskforce'. *The Guardian*, 1 December. Available at: **www. guardian.co.uk**

Latest 7 (2012) 'It all adds up'. *Latest 7*, 16 April. Available at: **http://thelatest.co.uk**

Lord Laming (2009) *The Protection of Children in England: A Progress Report.* London: The Stationery Office.

Munro, E (2011) *The Munro Review of Child Protection: Final Report. A child-centred system.* London: The Stationery Office.

Nelson-Jones, R (1988) *Practical Counselling and Helping Skills.* Second edition. London: Cassell Educational.

Oxford University Press (2011) *The Concise Oxford Dictionary: Main Edition*. Oxford: Oxford University Press.

Parker, J and Bradley, G (2010) *Social Work Practice: Assessment, Planning, Intervention and Review*. Third edition. Exeter: Learning Matters.

Payne, M (1991) *Modern Social Work Theory*. Basingstoke: Palgrave Macmillan.

Priestley, P and McGuire, J (1983) *Learning to Help: Basic Skills Exercises*. London and New York: Tavistock/Routledge.

Rozenberg, J (2012) 'Wigs off, jeans on at the Judicial College'. *The Guardian*, 8 February. Available at: **www.guardian.co.uk**

Rutter, L and Brown, K (2012) *Critical Thinking and Professional Judgement for Social Work*. Third edition. London: Sage/Learning Matters.

Samuel, M (2012) '"Vile" hate site faces legal action for naming social workers'. *Community Care*, 30 August. Available at: **www.communitycare.co.uk**

Seymour, C and Seymour, R (2011) *Courtroom and Report Writing Skills for Social Workers*. Second edition. Exeter: Learning Matters

Solebo, C, Sidebotham, P and Watson, C (2010) Preparing paediatricians for court: Evaluation of a court skills training programme. *Child Abuse Review*, 21(2): 131–40.

Stepney, P and Ford, D (2000) *Social Work Models, Methods and Theories*. Lyme Regis: Russell House Publishing.

Taggart, C and Wines, J (2008) *My Grammar and I*. London: Michael O'Mara Books.

Teater, B (2010) *An Introduction to Applying Social Work Theories and Methods*. Maidenhead: Open University Press.

Trevithick, P (2012) *Social Work Skills and Knowledge*. Third edition. Maidenhead: Open University Press.

Trinder, L with Reynolds, S (2000) *Evidence-Based Practice: A Critical Appraisal*. Oxford: Blackwell Science Ltd.

Truss, L (2003) *Eats, Shoots & Leaves*. London: HarperCollins.

Wacks, R (2008) *Law: A Very Short Introduction*. Oxford: Oxford University Press.

Walker, H (2011) *Studying for Your Social Work Degree*. Second edition. Exeter: Learning Matters.

Walker, H and Beaumont, B (1981) *Probation Work: Critical Theory and Socialist Practice*. Oxford: Basil Blackwell.

Walker, H and Beaumont, B (1985) *Working with Offenders*. Basingstoke: Macmillan.

Walker, S, Shemmings, D and Cleaver, H (2012) *Write Enough*. Available at: **www.writeenough.org.uk**

Index